# 50 Gourmet Mexican Dishes Recipes for Home

By: Kelly Johnson

# Table of Contents

- Tacos al Pastor
- Mole Poblano
- Enchiladas Suizas
- Chiles Rellenos
- Carnitas
- Pozole
- Sopes
- Tamales
- Cochinita Pibil
- Guacamole with Pomegranate
- Ceviche de Camarones
- Chilaquiles
- Shrimp and Avocado Tostadas
- Birria
- Tostadas de Tinga
- Queso Fundido with Chorizo
- Pescado a la Veracruzana
- Tacos de Pescado
- Rajas con Crema
- Elote en Vaso (Cup of Corn)
- Salsa Verde Chicken
- Tacos de Lengua
- Tostadas de Carnitas
- Nopales Salad
- Molletes
- Camarones a la Diabla
- Tlayudas
- Pibil-Style Salmon
- Guajillo Chicken Stew
- Huitlacoche Quesadillas
- Barbacoa
- Salsa Roja Shrimp
- Cochinita Pibil Tacos
- Alambre
- Mexican Street Corn Soup

- Tinga de Pollo
- Tacos de Birria
- Sopa de Lima
- Chicken Tinga Tostadas
- Huachinango a la Veracruzana (Veracruz-Style Red Snapper)
- Tacos de Carnitas con Salsa Verde
- Pescado Zarandeado
- Tacos de Rajas con Queso
- Pambazos
- Chorizo and Potato Tacos
- Chicken Chiles Rellenos
- Sopes de Tinga
- Tacos de Marlin
- Churros with Chocolate Dipping Sauce
- Capirotada (Mexican Bread Pudding)

**Tacos al Pastor**

Ingredients:

For the Marinade:

- 3 dried guajillo chilies, deseeded and soaked in hot water
- 2 dried ancho chilies, deseeded and soaked in hot water
- 1 small onion, roughly chopped
- 3 cloves garlic
- 1/4 cup white vinegar
- 1/4 cup pineapple juice
- 1 teaspoon dried oregano
- 1 teaspoon ground cumin
- 1 teaspoon smoked paprika
- 1 teaspoon achiote paste (optional, for color)
- Salt and pepper to taste

For the Tacos:

- 2 pounds pork shoulder, thinly sliced
- Corn tortillas
- Pineapple slices, diced
- Chopped fresh cilantro
- Diced onions
- Lime wedges

Instructions:

In a blender, combine all the marinade ingredients and blend until you get a smooth paste.
Marinate the thinly sliced pork shoulder in the prepared marinade. Cover and refrigerate for at least 2 hours, or preferably overnight for the best flavor.
Preheat your grill or a grill pan over medium-high heat.
Thread the marinated pork slices onto skewers, creating a vertical stack.
Grill the stacked pork slices on all sides until cooked through and slightly crispy, about 15-20 minutes.
While grilling, warm the corn tortillas on the grill.
Once the pork is cooked, remove it from the skewers and assemble your tacos.

Place a generous amount of grilled pork on each warm tortilla.
Top with diced pineapple, chopped cilantro, diced onions, and a squeeze of lime juice.
Serve immediately and enjoy your homemade Tacos al Pastor!

Feel free to customize your tacos with your favorite salsa or hot sauce. This recipe captures the essence of the traditional Tacos al Pastor found in Mexico, combining the smoky, spicy, and slightly sweet flavors for an authentic taste.

**Mole Poblano**

Ingredients:

For the Mole Sauce:

- 4 dried ancho chilies, stemmed and deseeded
- 3 dried guajillo chilies, stemmed and deseeded
- 2 dried pasilla chilies, stemmed and deseeded
- 1/4 cup sesame seeds
- 1/4 cup almonds
- 1/4 cup peanuts
- 1/4 cup raisins
- 1/4 cup pumpkin seeds (pepitas)
- 1/2 cup tortilla chips
- 1/2 cup stale bread, torn into pieces
- 1 onion, chopped
- 3 cloves garlic, minced
- 1 teaspoon ground cinnamon
- 1/2 teaspoon ground cloves
- 1/2 teaspoon ground cumin
- 1/2 teaspoon dried oregano
- 1/4 teaspoon black pepper
- 1/4 teaspoon coriander
- 3 tablespoons vegetable oil
- 4 cups chicken broth
- 2 tablets Mexican chocolate (Abuelita or Ibarra), chopped
- Salt to taste

For the Meat:

- 1 whole chicken, cut into serving pieces
- Salt and pepper to taste

Instructions:

Prepare the Chilies: Heat a dry skillet over medium heat and lightly toast the dried chilies until fragrant. Be careful not to burn them. Remove from heat and soak them in hot water for about 20-30 minutes until softened.

Prepare the Mole Paste: In a large skillet, heat 2 tablespoons of oil over medium heat. Add chopped onion and garlic and sauté until softened. Add sesame seeds, almonds, peanuts, raisins, pumpkin seeds, and torn bread. Toast until golden brown.

In a blender, combine the toasted mixture with the soaked chilies (drained), tortilla chips, cinnamon, cloves, cumin, oregano, black pepper, and coriander. Blend until smooth, adding chicken broth as needed to create a thick paste.

In the same skillet, heat the remaining oil over medium heat. Add the blended paste and cook, stirring constantly, for about 10-15 minutes until it thickens and deepens in color.

Gradually add the chicken broth, stirring constantly to avoid lumps. Once smooth, bring the mixture to a simmer.

Add the chopped chocolate and stir until melted. Season with salt to taste.

Simmer for an additional 15-20 minutes, stirring occasionally.

Prepare the Chicken: Season the chicken pieces with salt and pepper. In a separate pot, cook the chicken until fully cooked.

Serve the Mole Poblano over the cooked chicken pieces, and optionally, garnish with sesame seeds. This dish is traditionally served with rice or warm tortillas.

Mole Poblano is a labor of love, but the depth of flavors is well worth the effort. Adjust the spiciness and sweetness according to your taste preferences.

**Enchiladas Suizas**

Ingredients:

For the Filling:

- 2 cups shredded cooked chicken
- 1 cup diced onion
- 1 cup diced bell peppers (red and green)
- 1 clove garlic, minced
- Salt and pepper to taste
- 1 tablespoon vegetable oil

For the Green Salsa:

- 4 tomatillos, husked and washed
- 2 green jalapeños (adjust according to your spice preference)
- 1/2 cup chopped cilantro
- 1/2 cup sour cream
- Salt to taste

For the Assembly:

- 8-10 corn tortillas
- 1 cup shredded Mexican cheese blend

Instructions:

Preheat the oven to 375°F (190°C).
In a skillet, heat vegetable oil over medium heat. Add onions, bell peppers, and garlic. Cook until the vegetables are soft and onions are translucent.
Add shredded chicken to the skillet and season with salt and pepper. Mix well and cook for a few minutes until the chicken is heated through. Set aside.
To prepare the green salsa, in a blender, combine tomatillos, jalapeños, cilantro, sour cream, and salt. Blend until smooth.
Pour a small amount of the green salsa into the bottom of a baking dish to coat the surface.
Warm the corn tortillas in a dry skillet or microwave to make them pliable.
Spoon the chicken mixture onto each tortilla, roll them up, and place them seam-side down in the baking dish.

Pour the remaining green salsa over the enchiladas, ensuring they are well-covered.

Sprinkle shredded cheese over the top of the enchiladas.

Bake in the preheated oven for about 20-25 minutes or until the cheese is melted and bubbly.

Once done, remove from the oven and let them cool for a few minutes before serving.

Serve the Enchiladas Suizas with additional toppings like chopped cilantro, sliced jalapeños, and a dollop of sour cream if desired. Enjoy your flavorful and cheesy Mexican dish!

**Chiles Rellenos**

Ingredients:

For the Filling:

- 4 large poblano or Anaheim peppers
- 2 cups shredded cheese (queso fresco, Oaxaca, or a Mexican cheese blend)
- For a meat filling, you can use cooked and seasoned ground beef, shredded chicken, or pork

For the Batter:

- 4 large eggs, separated
- 1/2 cup all-purpose flour
- 1/2 teaspoon baking powder
- Salt to taste

For the Sauce:

- 2 cups tomato sauce
- 1/2 cup chicken or vegetable broth
- 1 clove garlic, minced
- 1 teaspoon dried oregano
- Salt and pepper to taste

For Frying:

- Vegetable oil for frying

Instructions:

Preheat the oven broiler. Place the whole poblano or Anaheim peppers on a baking sheet and broil, turning occasionally, until the skin is blistered and charred on all sides. This process usually takes about 10-15 minutes.

Transfer the roasted peppers to a bowl and cover it with plastic wrap. Let them steam for about 15 minutes. This will make it easier to peel off the skin.

Peel the skin off the peppers, make a small slit down one side, and carefully remove the seeds and membranes, leaving the stem intact.

Stuff each pepper with shredded cheese or your desired filling.

In a bowl, beat the egg whites until stiff peaks form. In a separate bowl, beat the egg yolks, then fold them into the egg whites.

In another bowl, mix together the flour, baking powder, and salt. Gently fold this mixture into the egg mixture until well combined.

Heat vegetable oil in a deep pan over medium-high heat.

Dip each stuffed pepper into the batter, making sure it's well-coated.

Carefully place the battered peppers into the hot oil, and fry until golden brown on all sides. This might be done in batches.

Once fried, place the Chiles Rellenos on a plate lined with paper towels to absorb excess oil.

For the sauce, combine tomato sauce, broth, minced garlic, oregano, salt, and pepper in a saucepan. Simmer for about 10 minutes.

Serve the Chiles Rellenos hot, drizzled with the tomato sauce.

Chiles Rellenos are often served with rice and beans. Garnish with chopped cilantro, sour cream, or sliced avocado if desired. Enjoy your delicious and flavorful Chiles Rellenos!

**Carnitas**

Ingredients:

- 3-4 pounds pork shoulder or pork butt, cut into large chunks
- 1 onion, coarsely chopped
- 4 cloves garlic, minced
- 1 orange, juiced
- 1 lime, juiced
- 1 teaspoon ground cumin
- 1 teaspoon dried oregano
- 1 teaspoon smoked paprika
- 1 teaspoon ground coriander
- Salt and pepper to taste
- 2 bay leaves
- 1 cup chicken broth

For Serving:

- Corn or flour tortillas
- Chopped cilantro
- Diced onions
- Salsa or pico de gallo
- Lime wedges

Instructions:

Preheat the Oven: Preheat your oven to 325°F (163°C).
Season the Pork: In a large bowl, combine the pork chunks, chopped onion, minced garlic, orange juice, lime juice, cumin, oregano, smoked paprika, coriander, salt, and pepper. Mix well to ensure the pork is evenly coated with the seasoning.
Marinate: Allow the pork to marinate for at least 30 minutes or, for better flavor, refrigerate it overnight.
Cooking: Transfer the marinated pork to a heavy oven-safe pot or Dutch oven. Add bay leaves and chicken broth.
Slow Cook: Cover the pot and place it in the preheated oven. Slow-cook the pork for about 2.5 to 3 hours or until the meat is tender and easily falls apart.

Crisping: Once the pork is tender, increase the oven temperature to 425°F (218°C). Uncover the pot and cook for an additional 20-30 minutes or until the top of the pork becomes crispy.

Shred the Meat: Remove the bay leaves and use two forks to shred the pork into smaller pieces. Mix it with the juices in the pot.

Serve: Warm the tortillas and fill them with the shredded carnitas. Top with chopped cilantro, diced onions, and salsa. Squeeze lime over the top.

Carnitas are versatile and can be used in tacos, burritos, nachos, or even served over rice. Enjoy the rich and flavorful taste of homemade carnitas!

**Pozole**

Ingredients:

For the Pozole:

- 1 pound dried hominy (maize pozolero), soaked overnight and cooked according to package instructions
- 3-4 pounds pork shoulder, cut into chunks
- 1 large onion, peeled and halved
- 4-5 cloves garlic, peeled
- 2 bay leaves
- Salt to taste

For the Red Chile Sauce:

- 4-5 dried guajillo chiles, stemmed and seeded
- 2-3 dried ancho chiles, stemmed and seeded
- 2 cloves garlic, peeled
- 1 teaspoon dried oregano
- 1 teaspoon ground cumin
- Salt to taste
- 1 cup chicken or pork broth (reserved from cooking the meat)

For Toppings:

- Shredded lettuce
- Radishes, sliced
- Chopped cilantro
- Diced onions
- Lime wedges

Instructions:

Prepare the Hominy: Soak the dried hominy overnight in plenty of water. Rinse and cook the hominy according to the package instructions until it's tender.

Cook the Meat: In a large pot, combine the pork chunks, halved onion, garlic cloves, bay leaves, and salt. Cover with water and bring to a boil. Reduce heat to a simmer and cook until the meat is tender, usually 2-3 hours.

Make the Red Chile Sauce: While the meat is cooking, prepare the red chile sauce. In a dry skillet, toast the dried chiles over medium heat for a few minutes until fragrant. Place them in a bowl, cover with hot water, and let them soak for about 15-20 minutes. Blend the soaked chiles with garlic, oregano, cumin, salt, and a cup of the broth from cooking the meat until you have a smooth sauce.

Shred the Meat: Once the meat is tender, remove the onion, garlic, and bay leaves. Shred the pork into smaller pieces.

Combine and Simmer: Add the cooked hominy and red chile sauce to the pot with the shredded meat. Bring the mixture to a simmer and let it cook for an additional 30 minutes to allow the flavors to meld.

Adjust Seasoning: Taste and adjust the seasoning as needed, adding more salt if necessary.

Serve: Ladle the pozole into bowls and serve with your choice of toppings, such as shredded lettuce, sliced radishes, chopped cilantro, diced onions, and lime wedges.

Pozole is often enjoyed as a hearty and comforting soup, especially during celebrations and gatherings. It's a dish with deep cultural significance in Mexican cuisine.

**Sopes**

Ingredients:

For the Sopes:

- 2 cups masa harina (corn masa flour)
- 1 1/4 cups warm water
- 1/2 teaspoon salt
- Vegetable oil for frying

For Toppings (adjust to your liking):

- Refried beans
- Cooked and shredded meat (chicken, beef, pork)
- Lettuce, shredded
- Salsa (red or green)
- Mexican crema or sour cream
- Queso fresco or shredded cheese
- Chopped tomatoes
- Chopped onions
- Chopped cilantro
- Sliced jalapeños (optional)

Instructions:

Prepare the Masa Dough:
- In a large mixing bowl, combine the masa harina and salt.
- Gradually add warm water while kneading until you achieve a soft and pliable dough.

Shape the Sopes:
- Take small portions of the dough and roll them into balls (about 2 inches in diameter).
- Flatten each ball into a thick disc (about 1/4 to 1/2 inch thick) with raised edges to form the sope.

Cook the Sopes:
- Heat a griddle or skillet over medium heat.
- Cook the sopes for a few minutes on each side until they are lightly browned and cooked through.

- Optionally, you can also fry the sopes in vegetable oil until they are golden brown and crispy.

Assemble the Sopes:
- Spread a layer of refried beans on each sope.
- Top with shredded meat, lettuce, salsa, crema, cheese, tomatoes, onions, cilantro, and any other toppings you prefer.

Serve and Enjoy:
- Arrange the sopes on a platter and serve immediately.

Feel free to get creative with the toppings and adjust the recipe to suit your taste. Sopes are meant to be a customizable and delicious dish!

**Tamales**

Ingredients:

For the Masa Dough:

- 3 cups masa harina
- 1 cup lard or vegetable shortening
- 1 teaspoon baking powder
- 1 teaspoon salt
- 2 to 2.5 cups chicken or pork broth (warm)

For the Pork Filling:

- 2 pounds pork shoulder or pork butt, cubed
- 1 onion, chopped
- 3 cloves garlic, minced
- 2 teaspoons ground cumin
- 1 teaspoon chili powder
- Salt and pepper to taste
- 1 cup red enchilada sauce (optional)

For Assembly:

- Corn husks, soaked in warm water
- Salsa verde or red salsa (for serving)

Instructions:

Preparing the Pork Filling:

In a large skillet, sauté the chopped onions and garlic until translucent.
Add the cubed pork and brown on all sides.
Season the pork with cumin, chili powder, salt, and pepper.
If using, pour the enchilada sauce over the pork and simmer until the meat is cooked through and tender. Set aside.

Making the Masa Dough:

In a large mixing bowl, beat the lard or shortening until fluffy.
In a separate bowl, combine the masa harina, baking powder, and salt.

Gradually add the masa harina mixture to the beaten lard, alternating with the warm chicken or pork broth. Mix until you achieve a soft, spreadable consistency.

Assembling the Tamales:

Take a soaked corn husk and spread a thin layer of the masa dough onto the center of the husk.
Add a spoonful of the pork filling in the center of the masa.
Fold the sides of the corn husk over the filling, then fold the top and bottom to encase the filling in a rectangular shape.
Repeat the process until all the masa and filling are used.

Steaming the Tamales:

Arrange the tamales in a steamer basket with the open end facing up.
Steam the tamales for about 1.5 to 2 hours or until the masa is cooked through and easily separates from the husk.
Allow the tamales to cool for a few minutes before serving.

Serving:

Unwrap the tamales and serve them with your favorite salsa (salsa verde or red salsa).

Enjoy your homemade pork tamales! You can also experiment with different fillings and flavors to suit your taste.

**Cochinita Pibil**

Ingredients:

For the Achiote Marinade:

- 3 tablespoons achiote paste
- 1/2 cup orange juice
- 1/4 cup white vinegar
- 3 cloves garlic, minced
- 1 teaspoon ground cumin
- 1 teaspoon oregano
- Salt and pepper to taste

For the Cochinita Pibil:

- 2-3 pounds pork shoulder or pork butt, cut into chunks
- Banana leaves (if available), for wrapping
- 1 red onion, thinly sliced
- 2 oranges, juice and zest
- 2 lemons, juice and zest
- Salt to taste
- Additional banana leaves for lining the cooking vessel (if using)

Instructions:

Prepare the Achiote Marinade:
- In a blender or food processor, combine all the ingredients for the achiote marinade. Blend until you have a smooth paste.

Marinate the Pork:
- Place the pork chunks in a large bowl and coat them thoroughly with the achiote marinade. Ensure the meat is well-covered. Allow it to marinate for at least 2 hours or preferably overnight in the refrigerator.

Prepare Banana Leaves (if using):
- If using banana leaves, briefly pass them over an open flame to make them pliable. This helps to enhance the flavor and makes them easier to handle.

Assemble and Wrap:
- Preheat your oven to 325°F (163°C).

- Lay out banana leaves or use a large, deep baking dish. If using banana leaves, line the bottom of the dish with them.
- Place the marinated pork in the dish, top it with sliced red onions, orange zest, lemon zest, and pour the orange and lemon juice over the meat.

Wrap and Cook:
- If using banana leaves, cover the pork with additional banana leaves and then tightly seal the dish with aluminum foil.
- Bake in the preheated oven for about 3-4 hours or until the pork is tender and easily shredded.

Serve:
- Once cooked, shred the pork with a fork. Serve the Cochinita Pibil with tortillas, pickled red onions, habanero salsa, and lime wedges.

Cochinita Pibil is often served as tacos or in tortas (sandwiches). The slow cooking and achiote marinade give the pork a distinctive and delicious flavor. Enjoy!

**Guacamole with Pomegranate**

Ingredients:

- 3 ripe avocados
- 1/2 cup pomegranate arils (seeds)
- 1/4 cup red onion, finely diced
- 1/4 cup fresh cilantro, chopped
- 1-2 small jalapeños, seeded and finely diced (adjust to your spice preference)
- 1-2 cloves garlic, minced
- Juice of 1-2 limes
- Salt and pepper to taste
- Optional: 1/2 teaspoon ground cumin for extra flavor

Instructions:

Prepare the Avocados:
- Cut the avocados in half, remove the pits, and scoop the flesh into a mixing bowl.

Mash the Avocados:
- Use a fork or potato masher to mash the avocados to your desired consistency. Some people prefer chunkier guacamole, while others like it smoother.

Add the Ingredients:
- Add the diced red onion, chopped cilantro, jalapeños, minced garlic, and pomegranate arils to the mashed avocados.

Season the Guacamole:
- Squeeze the juice of 1-2 limes into the mixture. Add salt, pepper, and ground cumin to taste. Mix well to combine.

Adjust Consistency and Flavor:
- If the guacamole is too thick, you can add more lime juice or a bit of water to reach your desired consistency. Taste and adjust the seasonings accordingly.

Serve:
- Transfer the guacamole to a serving bowl and garnish with additional pomegranate arils and cilantro if desired.

Enjoy:
- Serve the guacamole with tortilla chips, vegetable sticks, or as a topping for tacos, nachos, or any of your favorite dishes.

The pomegranate adds a sweet and juicy element to the guacamole, creating a unique flavor profile that pairs well with the creamy avocado. It's a colorful and delicious addition to your snack or party spread.

**Ceviche de Camarones**

Ingredients:

- 1 pound raw shrimp, peeled, deveined, and chopped into bite-sized pieces
- 1 cup fresh lime juice (about 8-10 limes)
- 1 cup fresh lemon juice (about 4-6 lemons)
- 1 medium red onion, finely diced
- 1 cucumber, peeled and diced
- 1-2 jalapeños, seeded and finely chopped
- 1 cup cherry tomatoes, halved
- 1/2 cup fresh cilantro, chopped
- 1 avocado, diced
- Salt and pepper to taste
- Tortilla chips or tostadas for serving

Instructions:

Prepare the Shrimp:
- Ensure the shrimp is cleaned, peeled, deveined, and chopped into bite-sized pieces.

Marinate the Shrimp:
- In a non-reactive bowl (glass or ceramic), combine the shrimp, lime juice, and lemon juice. Make sure the shrimp is fully submerged in the citrus juice. Cover the bowl and refrigerate for about 30 minutes to 1 hour, or until the shrimp turns opaque and appears "cooked."

Combine Ingredients:
- Drain excess citrus juice from the shrimp. Add diced red onion, cucumber, jalapeños, cherry tomatoes, and chopped cilantro to the shrimp. Mix gently to combine.

Season:
- Season the ceviche with salt and pepper to taste. Be mindful of the salt as the shrimp has already absorbed some from the citrus juice.

Add Avocado:
- Gently fold in the diced avocado. Be careful not to mash it; you want the avocado to remain in distinct pieces.

Chill:
- Cover the ceviche and refrigerate for an additional 15-30 minutes to let the flavors meld and allow the ceviche to chill.

Serve:

- Serve the Ceviche de Camarones in bowls or glasses, garnished with additional cilantro if desired. Accompany it with tortilla chips or tostadas for scooping.

Enjoy:
- Enjoy the fresh and zesty flavors of your shrimp ceviche!

Remember that the acidity of the citrus juices "cooks" the shrimp, but marination times can vary based on personal preference. Adjust the ingredients and spice levels according to your taste. This ceviche is perfect for a light and refreshing appetizer or a main dish on a warm day.

**Chilaquiles**

Ingredients:

For the Chilaquiles:

- 8-10 corn tortillas, cut into triangles or strips
- Vegetable oil for frying
- 2 cups salsa (red or green)
- 1 cup chicken or vegetable broth
- Salt to taste

For Toppings:

- 1 cup cooked and shredded chicken (optional)
- 1/2 cup crumbled queso fresco or cotija cheese
- 1/4 cup Mexican crema or sour cream
- Sliced avocado
- Chopped fresh cilantro
- Sliced radishes
- Fried or poached eggs (optional)

Instructions:

Fry the Tortillas:
- In a large skillet, heat enough vegetable oil to cover the bottom of the pan over medium-high heat. Fry the tortilla triangles or strips in batches until they are golden and crispy. Remove and place them on a paper towel-lined plate to drain excess oil.

Prepare the Sauce:
- In the same skillet, combine the salsa and chicken or vegetable broth. Simmer the mixture over medium heat for about 5-7 minutes, allowing it to thicken slightly. Season with salt to taste.

Combine Tortillas and Sauce:
- Add the fried tortillas to the sauce in the skillet. Gently toss to coat the tortillas evenly with the sauce. Cook for an additional 2-3 minutes, allowing the tortillas to absorb some of the sauce.

Add Toppings:
- Add the shredded chicken if using, crumbled queso fresco or cotija cheese, Mexican crema or sour cream, sliced avocado, chopped cilantro,

and sliced radishes. You can also add fried or poached eggs on top if desired.

Serve:
- Transfer the Chilaquiles to a serving platter. Garnish with additional toppings if desired.

Enjoy:
- Serve the Chilaquiles immediately while the tortillas are still crispy. They are often enjoyed as is or accompanied by refried beans on the side.

Chilaquiles are versatile, and you can customize them to your liking by adjusting the toppings and the type of salsa or sauce used. They're a delicious and satisfying dish that showcases the vibrant flavors of Mexican cuisine.

**Shrimp and Avocado Tostadas**

Ingredients:

For the Shrimp:

- 1 pound large shrimp, peeled and deveined
- 2 tablespoons olive oil
- 2 cloves garlic, minced
- 1 teaspoon chili powder
- Salt and pepper to taste
- Juice of 1 lime

For the Avocado Mash:

- 2 ripe avocados
- Juice of 1 lime
- Salt and pepper to taste

For Assembly:

- Tostada shells (store-bought or homemade)
- 1 cup shredded lettuce
- 1 cup diced tomatoes
- 1/2 cup red onion, finely chopped
- Fresh cilantro, chopped
- Optional: Salsa or hot sauce for extra flavor

Instructions:

Prepare the Shrimp:
- In a bowl, combine the shrimp with olive oil, minced garlic, chili powder, salt, pepper, and lime juice. Toss to coat the shrimp evenly.
- Heat a skillet over medium-high heat. Cook the shrimp for 2-3 minutes per side or until they are opaque and cooked through. Remove from heat.

Make the Avocado Mash:
- In a separate bowl, mash the ripe avocados with lime juice until smooth. Season with salt and pepper to taste.

Assemble the Tostadas:
- Spread a generous layer of the avocado mash onto each tostada shell.

Add Shrimp:
- Top the avocado mash with the cooked shrimp.

Add Toppings:
- Layer on shredded lettuce, diced tomatoes, and chopped red onion.

Garnish:
- Sprinkle with fresh cilantro and add salsa or hot sauce if desired.

Serve:
- Arrange the Shrimp and Avocado Tostadas on a serving platter and serve immediately.

Enjoy:
- Enjoy these tasty tostadas with a burst of flavors and textures from the creamy avocado, savory shrimp, and fresh toppings.

Feel free to customize the toppings based on your preferences. You can also add a drizzle of crema or Mexican sour cream for an extra layer of richness. These tostadas make for a perfect appetizer, light lunch, or a flavorful dinner option.

**Birria**

Ingredients:

For the Birria:

- 3-4 pounds beef stew meat (such as chuck roast), cut into chunks
- 2-3 dried guajillo chilies, stemmed and seeded
- 2-3 dried ancho chilies, stemmed and seeded
- 1 medium onion, chopped
- 4 cloves garlic, minced
- 1 teaspoon dried oregano
- 1 teaspoon ground cumin
- 1/2 teaspoon ground cloves
- 4 cups beef broth
- 1 cup tomato sauce
- Salt and pepper to taste
- 2 bay leaves

For Serving:

- Corn tortillas
- Chopped fresh cilantro
- Diced onions
- Lime wedges
- Salsa or hot sauce (optional)

Instructions:

Prepare the Chilies:
- Toast the dried guajillo and ancho chilies in a dry skillet over medium heat for a few seconds on each side until they become fragrant. Remove from heat, then soak them in hot water for about 15-20 minutes until softened.

Make the Chili Sauce:
- In a blender, combine the soaked chilies, chopped onion, minced garlic, oregano, ground cumin, ground cloves, and a small amount of water. Blend until you have a smooth, thick sauce.

Brown the Meat:
- Season the beef chunks with salt and pepper. In a large pot or Dutch oven, heat a bit of oil over medium-high heat. Brown the meat on all sides.

Add the Chili Sauce:
- Pour the chili sauce over the browned meat in the pot. Stir to coat the meat evenly.

Add Liquids and Simmer:
- Pour in the beef broth, add the tomato sauce, and drop in the bay leaves. Bring the mixture to a boil, then reduce the heat to low, cover, and simmer for 2-3 hours or until the meat is tender and easily falls apart.

Serve:
- Serve the Birria with warm corn tortillas. Garnish with chopped cilantro, diced onions, and lime wedges. Optionally, offer salsa or hot sauce on the side.

Enjoy:
- Enjoy the rich and flavorful Birria, either by dipping the tortillas into the broth or making birria tacos by stuffing the meat into the tortillas with your preferred toppings.

Birria is often enjoyed as a celebratory dish and is commonly served during special occasions or family gatherings. The slow cooking process and aromatic spices create a dish that is both comforting and delicious.

**Tostadas de Tinga**

Ingredients:

For the Tinga:

- 2 cups cooked and shredded chicken or pork
- 2 tablespoons vegetable oil
- 1 onion, thinly sliced
- 2 cloves garlic, minced
- 1 can (14 ounces) diced tomatoes
- 2-3 chipotle peppers in adobo sauce, chopped
- 1 teaspoon dried oregano
- 1/2 teaspoon ground cumin
- Salt and pepper to taste

For the Tostadas:

- Tostada shells (store-bought or homemade)
- Refried beans (optional)
- Shredded lettuce
- Diced tomatoes
- Sliced avocado
- Mexican crema or sour cream
- Crumbled queso fresco or cotija cheese
- Fresh cilantro, chopped
- Lime wedges

Instructions:

Prepare the Tinga:
- In a large skillet, heat the vegetable oil over medium heat. Add the sliced onion and sauté until softened.
- Add the minced garlic and cook for another 1-2 minutes until fragrant.
- Stir in the shredded chicken or pork and cook for a few minutes to brown slightly.

Add Sauce:
- Add the diced tomatoes, chipotle peppers, oregano, cumin, salt, and pepper to the skillet. Mix well to combine.

- Simmer the tinga mixture over medium-low heat for about 15-20 minutes, allowing the flavors to meld and the sauce to thicken.

Prepare Tostadas:
- If desired, spread a thin layer of refried beans on each tostada shell.

Assemble Tostadas:
- Top each tostada with a generous portion of the tinga mixture.

Add Toppings:
- Garnish with shredded lettuce, diced tomatoes, sliced avocado, Mexican crema or sour cream, crumbled queso fresco or cotija cheese, and chopped cilantro.

Serve:
- Arrange the Tostadas de Tinga on a serving platter and serve with lime wedges on the side.

Enjoy:
- Enjoy the Tostadas de Tinga as a flavorful and satisfying meal. Serve them as an appetizer, snack, or part of a larger Mexican feast.

Feel free to customize the toppings based on your preferences. Tostadas de Tinga are known for their bold flavors and are sure to be a hit with anyone who loves Mexican cuisine.

**Queso Fundido with Chorizo**

Ingredients:

- 1 tablespoon vegetable oil
- 1/2 pound (about 225g) chorizo sausage, casing removed
- 1 small onion, finely chopped
- 2 cloves garlic, minced
- 2 cups shredded melting cheese (such as Oaxaca, Chihuahua, or a blend of Monterey Jack and mozzarella)
- 1 cup shredded sharp cheddar cheese
- 1/2 cup diced tomatoes (optional, for garnish)
- 1/4 cup chopped fresh cilantro (optional, for garnish)
- Warm tortillas or crusty bread for serving

Instructions:

Preheat the Oven:
- Preheat your oven to 375°F (190°C).

Cook the Chorizo:
- In a skillet over medium heat, heat the vegetable oil. Add the chorizo, breaking it up with a spoon, and cook until it's browned and cooked through. Remove any excess grease.

Add Aromatics:
- Add the chopped onion and minced garlic to the chorizo. Cook for a few minutes until the onion is softened.

Melt the Cheese:
- In an oven-safe dish or a cast-iron skillet, combine the shredded melting cheese and cheddar cheese. Transfer the skillet or dish to the preheated oven.

Bake:
- Bake for about 8-10 minutes or until the cheese is fully melted and bubbly, with a golden-brown top.

Combine with Chorizo:
- Carefully remove the dish from the oven. Spoon the cooked chorizo, onion, and garlic mixture over the melted cheese. Gently stir to combine.

Garnish:
- If desired, garnish the Queso Fundido with diced tomatoes and chopped cilantro.

Serve:

- Serve the Queso Fundido with warm tortillas or slices of crusty bread for dipping.

Enjoy:
- Enjoy this gooey and flavorful Queso Fundido with Chorizo as a delicious appetizer or snack.

This dish is perfect for sharing with friends or family during gatherings. The combination of melted cheese and savory chorizo creates a satisfying and comforting treat. Adjust the spice level by choosing your preferred type of chorizo.

**Pescado a la Veracruzana**

Ingredients:

- 4 fillets of white fish (such as red snapper or tilapia)
- Salt and pepper to taste
- 1/4 cup all-purpose flour (for dusting the fish)
- 2 tablespoons vegetable oil
- 1 onion, thinly sliced
- 2 cloves garlic, minced
- 1 bell pepper, thinly sliced (preferably red or green)
- 1 can (14 ounces) diced tomatoes, undrained
- 1/4 cup green olives, sliced
- 2 tablespoons capers
- 1 teaspoon dried oregano
- 1 teaspoon dried thyme
- 1 bay leaf
- 1/2 cup white wine or fish stock
- Fresh cilantro or parsley for garnish
- Lime wedges for serving

Instructions:

Prepare the Fish:
- Season the fish fillets with salt and pepper. Dust each fillet lightly with flour, shaking off any excess.

Sear the Fish:
- In a large skillet, heat the vegetable oil over medium-high heat. Sear the fish fillets on both sides until golden brown. Remove the fish from the skillet and set aside.

Sauté Aromatics:
- In the same skillet, add a bit more oil if needed. Sauté the thinly sliced onion, minced garlic, and bell pepper until softened.

Create the Tomato Sauce:
- Add the diced tomatoes with their juices to the skillet. Stir in the green olives, capers, dried oregano, dried thyme, and the bay leaf. Pour in the white wine or fish stock, and bring the mixture to a simmer.

Simmer:
- Allow the sauce to simmer for about 10-15 minutes, allowing the flavors to meld and the sauce to thicken slightly.

Add the Fish:
- Gently place the seared fish fillets back into the skillet, nestling them into the sauce. Spoon some of the sauce over the top of the fish.

Finish Cooking:
- Cover the skillet and let the fish simmer in the sauce for an additional 10-15 minutes, or until the fish is cooked through and flakes easily with a fork.

Garnish and Serve:
- Remove the bay leaf. Garnish with fresh cilantro or parsley. Serve the Pescado a la Veracruzana with lime wedges on the side.

Enjoy:
- Serve this delicious fish dish over rice or with crusty bread, enjoying the vibrant flavors of the Veracruzana-style sauce.

Pescado a la Veracruzana is known for its bold flavors, combining the sweetness of tomatoes, the brininess of olives and capers, and the freshness of herbs. It's a delightful dish that represents the coastal culinary traditions of Veracruz.

**Tacos de Pescado**

Ingredients:

For the Battered Fish:

- 1 pound white fish fillets (such as cod or tilapia), cut into strips
- 1 cup all-purpose flour
- 1 teaspoon baking powder
- 1 teaspoon ground cumin
- 1/2 teaspoon chili powder
- 1/2 teaspoon paprika
- 1 cup cold sparkling water
- Salt and pepper to taste
- Vegetable oil for frying

For Assembly:

- Corn or flour tortillas
- Shredded cabbage or lettuce
- Pico de gallo or salsa fresca
- Sliced radishes
- Fresh cilantro, chopped
- Lime wedges
- Crema or Mexican sour cream (optional)

Instructions:

Prepare the Battered Fish:
- In a bowl, whisk together the flour, baking powder, cumin, chili powder, paprika, salt, and pepper.
- Gradually add the cold sparkling water, whisking continuously until you have a smooth batter.

Batter and Fry the Fish:
- Dip the fish fillets into the batter, ensuring they are evenly coated.
- In a deep skillet or frying pan, heat vegetable oil over medium-high heat.
- Fry the battered fish strips for 2-3 minutes on each side or until golden brown and crispy. Place them on a paper towel-lined plate to absorb any excess oil.

Assemble the Tacos:

- Warm the tortillas in a dry skillet or microwave.
- Place a portion of the fried fish on each tortilla.

Add Garnishes:
- Top the fish with shredded cabbage or lettuce, pico de gallo or salsa fresca, sliced radishes, and chopped cilantro.

Drizzle with Sauce:
- Drizzle with crema or Mexican sour cream if desired.

Serve:
- Serve the Tacos de Pescado with lime wedges on the side.

Enjoy:
- Enjoy these delicious fish tacos immediately, savoring the combination of crispy fish, fresh toppings, and the tangy kick from lime.

Feel free to customize the toppings and sauces based on your preferences. Tacos de Pescado are a delightful and versatile dish, perfect for a casual meal or entertaining guests.

**Rajas con Crema**

Ingredients:

For the Fish:

- 1 pound white fish fillets (such as cod or tilapia)
- 1/2 cup all-purpose flour
- 1 teaspoon chili powder
- 1/2 teaspoon cumin
- Salt and pepper to taste
- Vegetable oil for frying

For the Cabbage Slaw:

- 2 cups shredded green cabbage
- 1/4 cup chopped fresh cilantro
- 1 tablespoon mayonnaise
- 1 tablespoon lime juice
- Salt and pepper to taste

For Assembly:

- Corn tortillas
- Sliced radishes
- Avocado slices
- Lime wedges
- Hot sauce (optional)

Instructions:

Prepare the Fish:
- In a bowl, mix together the flour, chili powder, cumin, salt, and pepper. Coat each fish fillet with the flour mixture.

Fry the Fish:
- Heat vegetable oil in a pan over medium-high heat. Fry the fish fillets for 3-4 minutes on each side or until golden and cooked through. Place them on a paper towel-lined plate to absorb excess oil.

Make the Cabbage Slaw:
- In a separate bowl, combine the shredded cabbage, chopped cilantro, mayonnaise, lime juice, salt, and pepper. Toss to coat the cabbage evenly.

Assemble the Tacos:
- Warm the corn tortillas. Place a few pieces of fried fish on each tortilla.

- Top with the cabbage slaw, sliced radishes, and avocado slices.

Serve:
- Serve the fish tacos with lime wedges and hot sauce on the side.

Enjoy:
- Enjoy your Tacos de Pescado with the fresh and zesty flavors of the cabbage slaw!

## Rajas con Crema

Ingredients:

- 4 poblano peppers, roasted, peeled, and sliced into strips (rajas)
- 1 tablespoon vegetable oil
- 1 large onion, thinly sliced
- 2 cloves garlic, minced
- 1 cup Mexican crema or sour cream
- 1 cup shredded Oaxaca or Monterey Jack cheese
- Salt and pepper to taste
- Fresh cilantro, chopped (for garnish)
- Warm tortillas for serving

Instructions:

Prepare the Poblano Peppers:
- Roast the poblano peppers until the skin is charred. Place them in a plastic bag for a few minutes to steam, making it easier to peel off the skin. Remove the seeds and slice the peppers into strips (rajas).

Sauté Onions and Garlic:
- In a skillet, heat vegetable oil over medium heat. Add the thinly sliced onions and sauté until softened. Add minced garlic and cook for an additional minute.

Add Poblano Strips:
- Stir in the poblano pepper strips (rajas) and cook for a few minutes until everything is well combined.

Combine with Cream:
- Pour in the Mexican crema or sour cream and mix well. Allow the mixture to simmer for a few minutes until heated through.

Melt Cheese:
- Add the shredded cheese and stir until melted and creamy. Season with salt and pepper to taste.

Garnish and Serve:
- Garnish with chopped fresh cilantro. Serve the Rajas con Crema with warm tortillas.

Enjoy:
- Enjoy this creamy and mildly spicy dish as a taco filling or as a side dish.

Both Tacos de Pescado and Rajas con Crema are flavorful and popular dishes in Mexican cuisine. Enjoy these delicious recipes!

**Elote en Vaso (Cup of Corn)**

Ingredients:

- 4 ears of corn, husked and cleaned
- 1/2 cup mayonnaise
- 1/2 cup sour cream
- 1 cup crumbled cotija cheese (or feta cheese)
- 1 teaspoon chili powder (adjust to taste)
- 1/2 teaspoon paprika
- 1 lime, cut into wedges
- Fresh cilantro, chopped (optional)
- Hot sauce (optional)
- Salt to taste

Instructions:

Prepare the Corn:
- Grill or boil the corn until it's cooked through and has a slight char. If boiling, you can add a pinch of salt to the water for extra flavor.

Mix the Sauce:
- In a small bowl, mix together the mayonnaise and sour cream to create the sauce.

Coat the Corn:
- Once the corn is cooked, brush each ear with the mayo-sour cream sauce, ensuring it's evenly coated.

Sprinkle with Cheese and Seasonings:
- Roll the corn in crumbled cotija cheese (or feta cheese) to coat it well. Sprinkle chili powder, paprika, and a pinch of salt over the cheese-covered corn.

Serve in Cups:
- Place each corn on the cob in a cup or glass to make it easier to handle.

Garnish:
- Squeeze lime wedges over the corn. Optionally, sprinkle with fresh chopped cilantro and add hot sauce according to your spice preference.

Enjoy:
- Serve Elote en Vaso immediately while it's warm. Hold the cup from the bottom and enjoy the delicious combination of flavors.

Elote en Vaso is a delightful treat that captures the essence of Mexican street food. The combination of creamy mayo-sour cream sauce, tangy cotija cheese, and the smokiness of chili powder creates a savory and satisfying dish.

**Salsa Verde Chicken**

Ingredients:

- 1.5 to 2 pounds boneless, skinless chicken thighs or breasts
- Salt and pepper to taste
- 2 tablespoons vegetable oil
- 1 onion, finely chopped
- 2 cloves garlic, minced
- 1 jar (about 16 ounces) salsa verde (store-bought or homemade)
- 1 teaspoon ground cumin
- 1/2 teaspoon dried oregano
- 1/4 teaspoon cayenne pepper (optional, for extra heat)
- 1/2 cup chicken broth or water
- Fresh cilantro, chopped (for garnish)
- Lime wedges (for serving)

Instructions:

Season and Brown the Chicken:
- Season the chicken with salt and pepper. In a large skillet or Dutch oven, heat the vegetable oil over medium-high heat. Brown the chicken on all sides until golden. This step is to sear the chicken and add flavor.

Saute Onions and Garlic:
- Add finely chopped onions to the skillet and sauté until they are softened. Add minced garlic and cook for another minute until fragrant.

Add Salsa Verde:
- Pour the salsa verde over the chicken and onions. Stir to coat the chicken in the salsa.

Season and Simmer:
- Sprinkle ground cumin, dried oregano, and cayenne pepper (if using) over the chicken. Pour in chicken broth or water. Stir to combine. Bring the mixture to a simmer.

Cook the Chicken:
- Cover the skillet or Dutch oven and let the chicken simmer for about 20-25 minutes, or until the chicken is cooked through and tender.

Shred the Chicken:
- Once the chicken is cooked, use two forks to shred it directly in the skillet. The chicken should easily fall apart and absorb the flavorful salsa.

Serve:

- Garnish the Salsa Verde Chicken with chopped fresh cilantro. Serve it over rice, in tacos, burritos, or use it as a filling for enchiladas.

Enjoy:
- Serve with lime wedges on the side. Enjoy the Salsa Verde Chicken with your preferred accompaniment.

This Salsa Verde Chicken is not only delicious but also versatile. Feel free to customize it with additional toppings like shredded cheese, diced tomatoes, or avocado slices. It's a perfect dish for a quick and flavorful weeknight dinner.

**Tacos de Lengua**

Ingredients:

For Cooking the Beef Tongue:

- 1 beef tongue (about 2-3 pounds)
- 1 onion, quartered
- 3 cloves garlic, smashed
- 2 bay leaves
- Salt and pepper to taste

For Tacos:

- Cooked and shredded beef tongue
- Corn tortillas
- Finely chopped onion
- Chopped fresh cilantro
- Lime wedges
- Salsa or hot sauce (optional)

Instructions:

Prepare the Beef Tongue:
- Rinse the beef tongue under cold water. Place it in a large pot and cover it with water.
- Add quartered onion, smashed garlic, bay leaves, salt, and pepper to the pot.

Cook the Beef Tongue:
- Bring the water to a boil, then reduce the heat to low and simmer for about 2.5 to 3 hours or until the tongue is tender. The cooking time may vary, so check for tenderness by inserting a fork into the tongue.

Peel and Shred the Tongue:
- Once the tongue is tender, remove it from the pot and let it cool slightly. Peel off the outer skin (it should peel off easily). Shred the meat with two forks.

Warm the Tortillas:
- Heat the corn tortillas in a dry skillet or directly over a gas flame until they are warm and pliable.

Assemble the Tacos:

- Place a portion of the shredded beef tongue onto each warm tortilla.

Add Toppings:
- Top the tacos with finely chopped onion and fresh cilantro.

Serve:
- Serve the Tacos de Lengua with lime wedges on the side. Optionally, offer salsa or hot sauce for extra flavor.

Enjoy:
- Enjoy these flavorful and tender Beef Tongue Tacos with your favorite toppings.

Tacos de Lengua may sound unconventional, but the slow-cooked beef tongue results in a unique and delicious taco filling. The combination of the tender meat, onions, cilantro, and lime creates a mouthwatering taco experience. Adjust the toppings according to your taste preferences.

**Tostadas de Carnitas**

Ingredients:

For Carnitas:

- 2 lbs pork shoulder, cut into chunks
- 1 onion, chopped
- 4 cloves garlic, minced
- 1 orange, juiced
- 1 lime, juiced
- 1 tsp ground cumin
- 1 tsp dried oregano
- Salt and pepper to taste
- 2 tbsp vegetable oil

For Tostadas:

- Corn tortillas
- Vegetable oil for frying

Toppings:

- Shredded lettuce
- Diced tomatoes
- Salsa or pico de gallo
- Avocado slices or guacamole
- Sour cream
- Fresh cilantro, chopped
- Lime wedges

Instructions:

Prepare the Carnitas:
- Season the pork chunks with salt, pepper, cumin, and oregano.
- In a large pot or Dutch oven, heat vegetable oil over medium-high heat. Brown the pork pieces on all sides.

- Add chopped onion and minced garlic, sauté until fragrant.
- Pour in the orange and lime juice, scraping the bottom of the pot to release any flavorful bits.
- Reduce heat to low, cover, and let it simmer for 2-3 hours or until the pork is tender and easily shreddable.
- Shred the pork using two forks and let it cook uncovered for an additional 15-20 minutes until it gets crispy edges.

Prepare the Tostadas:
- Heat about 1 inch of vegetable oil in a skillet over medium-high heat.
- Fry the corn tortillas one at a time until they are golden brown and crispy. Use tongs to flip them to ensure both sides are cooked evenly.
- Place the fried tortillas on paper towels to drain excess oil.

Assemble the Tostadas:
- Spread a generous portion of carnitas on each tostada.
- Top with shredded lettuce, diced tomatoes, salsa or pico de gallo, avocado slices or guacamole, and a dollop of sour cream.
- Garnish with chopped cilantro and serve with lime wedges on the side.

Enjoy:
- Serve the tostadas de carnitas immediately while the tortillas are still crispy and the carnitas are hot. Enjoy this flavorful and satisfying Mexican dish!

Feel free to customize the toppings according to your preference, and you can also add extras like shredded cheese or pickled jalapeños for an extra kick.

**Nopales Salad**

Ingredients:

- 2 medium-sized nopales (prickly pear cactus pads)
- 1 cup cherry tomatoes, halved
- 1/2 red onion, thinly sliced
- 1/2 cup fresh cilantro, chopped
- 1 avocado, diced
- 1 jalapeño, seeded and finely chopped (optional for some heat)
- 2 tablespoons olive oil
- 1 lime, juiced
- Salt and pepper to taste
- Queso fresco or feta cheese, crumbled (optional for garnish)

Instructions:

Prepare the Nopales:
- Using a pair of tongs, hold each nopal pad over an open flame or a hot skillet for a few seconds to remove the thorns. Be cautious while handling nopales, as they can be prickly.
- Rinse the nopales under cold water and scrape off any remaining thorns with a knife.
- Slice the nopales into thin strips or bite-sized pieces.

Cook the Nopales:
- In a pot of boiling water, blanch the sliced nopales for about 5-7 minutes until they become tender. Drain and rinse under cold water to stop the cooking process.

Assemble the Salad:
- In a large bowl, combine the blanched nopales, cherry tomatoes, red onion, cilantro, diced avocado, and chopped jalapeño (if using).

Make the Dressing:
- In a small bowl, whisk together olive oil, lime juice, salt, and pepper to taste. Adjust the seasoning according to your preference.

Combine and Toss:
- Pour the dressing over the salad ingredients and gently toss everything together until well coated.

Chill and Garnish:

- Allow the nopales salad to chill in the refrigerator for at least 30 minutes to let the flavors meld.
- Optionally, garnish with crumbled queso fresco or feta cheese before serving.

Serve:
- Serve the nopales salad as a side dish or a light and healthy main course. It's a perfect accompaniment to grilled meats or as a topping for tacos.

This nopales salad is not only delicious but also packed with vitamins and minerals, making it a nutritious addition to your meals. Adjust the ingredients and seasoning to suit your taste preferences.

**Molletes**

Ingredients:

- 4 bolillo rolls or a French baguette, sliced in half
- 1 can (16 oz) refried beans
- 2 cups shredded cheese (commonly used: Oaxaca, Chihuahua, or Monterey Jack)
- Pico de gallo (diced tomatoes, onions, cilantro, and jalapeños)
- Guacamole (optional)
- Sliced jalapeños (optional)
- Salt and pepper to taste

Instructions:

Preheat the Oven:
- Preheat your oven to 375°F (190°C).

Prepare the Bolillo Rolls:
- Slice the bolillo rolls or French baguette in half lengthwise, creating two halves for each roll.

Toast the Bread:
- Place the halved rolls on a baking sheet, cut side up. Toast them in the preheated oven until the edges become crispy but not too hard.

Warm the Refried Beans:
- In a saucepan, heat the refried beans over medium heat. You can add a little water or oil to achieve your desired consistency. Season with salt and pepper to taste.

Spread Beans on Toasted Rolls:
- Spread a generous amount of warm refried beans onto each toasted half.

Add Cheese:
- Sprinkle a generous amount of shredded cheese over the beans, covering the surface.

Bake until Cheese Melts:
- Place the baking sheet back in the oven and bake until the cheese is melted and bubbly, usually for about 5-7 minutes.

Top with Toppings:
- Remove the molletes from the oven. Top each mollete with pico de gallo, guacamole (if using), and sliced jalapeños for some extra heat.

Serve:

- Serve the molletes immediately while they are warm. They are perfect for breakfast, brunch, or as a delicious and satisfying snack.

Feel free to customize your molletes by adding other toppings such as sour cream, salsa, or your favorite hot sauce. Molletes are versatile and can be enjoyed in various ways, making them a beloved and easy-to-make Mexican comfort food.

**Camarones a la Diabla**

Ingredients:

- 1 pound large shrimp, peeled and deveined
- 4 dried guajillo chilies, stems and seeds removed
- 2 dried arbol chilies (adjust for desired spice level)
- 3 tomatoes, chopped
- 1/2 medium onion, finely chopped
- 4 cloves garlic, minced
- 1/4 cup tomato paste
- 1 cup chicken or vegetable broth
- 2 tablespoons vegetable oil
- 1 teaspoon dried oregano
- 1/2 teaspoon cumin powder
- Salt and pepper to taste
- Lime wedges and chopped cilantro for garnish

Instructions:

Prepare the Chilies:
- Heat a dry skillet over medium heat and toast the dried guajillo and arbol chilies for about 1-2 minutes until they become fragrant. Be careful not to burn them.
- Soak the toasted chilies in hot water for 15-20 minutes or until they are softened.

Make the Chili Sauce:
- In a blender, combine the softened chilies, chopped tomatoes, minced garlic, tomato paste, oregano, cumin, and a pinch of salt. Blend until you achieve a smooth sauce. You can add a bit of the soaking water to help with the blending process.

Sauté Onions:
- In a large skillet or pan, heat vegetable oil over medium heat. Add finely chopped onions and cook until they become translucent.

Add the Chili Sauce:
- Pour the blended chili sauce into the skillet with onions. Cook and stir for about 5-7 minutes until the sauce thickens and the flavors meld.

Add Broth:

- Pour in the chicken or vegetable broth, stirring to combine. Simmer for an additional 5 minutes.

Cook the Shrimp:
- Add the peeled and deveined shrimp to the skillet. Cook for 5-7 minutes or until the shrimp turn opaque and are cooked through. Adjust the seasoning with salt and pepper.

Serve:
- Once the shrimp are cooked, remove the skillet from heat. Serve the Camarones a la Diabla over rice or with warm tortillas. Garnish with lime wedges and chopped cilantro.

Enjoy these spicy and flavorful Camarones a la Diabla with the vibrant taste of the chili sauce. Adjust the amount of arbol chilies according to your desired level of spiciness.

**Tlayudas**

Ingredients:

For the Tlayudas:

- Large tortillas (you can use store-bought or make your own)
- 1 cup refried black beans
- 2 cups Oaxaca cheese or shredded mozzarella
- 1 large tomato, sliced
- 1 avocado, sliced
- 1 cup shredded lettuce or cabbage
- 1/2 cup radishes, thinly sliced
- 1/4 cup fresh cilantro, chopped
- Optional: Sliced jalapeños for some heat

For the Asiento (pork lard spread):

- 1/2 cup pork lard
- 1 tablespoon dried oregano
- Salt to taste

Instructions:

Prepare the Asiento:
- In a small saucepan, melt the pork lard over low heat. Stir in the dried oregano and a pinch of salt. Cook for a few minutes until the oregano is fragrant. Set aside.

Prepare the Toppings:
- Slice the tomatoes, avocado, radishes, and chop the cilantro. Have the shredded lettuce or cabbage ready.

Assemble the Tlayudas:
- Heat a large griddle or skillet over medium-high heat.
- Place a tortilla on the griddle and heat it for a minute or two on each side until it becomes slightly crispy.

Spread the Refried Beans:
- Spread a layer of refried black beans on one side of the tortilla.

Add Cheese:
- Sprinkle a generous amount of Oaxaca cheese or shredded mozzarella over the beans.

Finish Toppings:
- Add slices of tomato and avocado, shredded lettuce or cabbage, and radishes. Optionally, add sliced jalapeños for extra heat.

Fold and Heat:
- If your tortilla is large, you can fold it in half. Place the tlayuda back on the griddle and cook until the cheese is melted, and the toppings are heated through.

Spread Asiento:
- Once off the heat, spread a thin layer of the prepared asiento (pork lard with oregano) on top of the tlayuda.

Garnish and Serve:
- Sprinkle chopped cilantro on top and serve the tlayudas whole or sliced into wedges.

Tlayudas are often enjoyed as a meal on their own, and you can customize the toppings based on your preferences. They are a delicious and versatile dish, perfect for sharing with friends and family.

**Pibil-Style Salmon**

Ingredients:

For the Marinade:

- 4 salmon fillets
- 1/2 cup achiote paste
- 3 tablespoons orange juice
- 2 tablespoons lime juice
- 3 cloves garlic, minced
- 1 teaspoon ground cumin
- 1 teaspoon dried oregano
- 1 teaspoon paprika
- Salt and pepper to taste

For Wrapping and Cooking:

- Banana leaves (if available) or parchment paper
- 1 red onion, thinly sliced
- 1 bell pepper, thinly sliced
- Fresh cilantro for garnish
- Lime wedges for serving

Instructions:

Prepare the Marinade:
- In a bowl, mix together achiote paste, orange juice, lime juice, minced garlic, ground cumin, dried oregano, paprika, salt, and pepper. Ensure the achiote paste is well incorporated into the marinade.

Marinate the Salmon:
- Place the salmon fillets in a dish or a resealable plastic bag. Pour the marinade over the salmon, ensuring each fillet is well coated. Allow it to marinate for at least 30 minutes to an hour in the refrigerator.

Preheat the Oven:
- Preheat your oven to 350°F (175°C).

Prepare the Wrapping:

- If using banana leaves, briefly pass them over an open flame to soften and make them pliable. Cut into large squares. If using parchment paper, cut into squares large enough to wrap each salmon fillet.

Assemble the Packets:
- Place a square of banana leaf or parchment paper on a flat surface. Put a few slices of red onion and bell pepper in the center. Lay a marinated salmon fillet on top and spoon some additional marinade over it. Add more onion and bell pepper slices on top.

Wrap the Packets:
- Fold the banana leaf or parchment paper around the salmon, creating a neat packet. Secure with kitchen twine if needed.

Bake in the Oven:
- Place the wrapped salmon packets on a baking sheet and bake in the preheated oven for about 20-25 minutes or until the salmon is cooked through.

Serve:
- Carefully open the packets, and transfer the salmon onto serving plates. Garnish with fresh cilantro and serve with lime wedges on the side.

This Pibil-Style Salmon has a wonderful blend of flavors from the achiote paste, citrus juices, and aromatic spices. It's a unique and delicious way to enjoy salmon with a Mexican twist. Serve it with rice, tortillas, or your favorite side dishes.

**Guajillo Chicken Stew**

Ingredients:

- 2 lbs chicken pieces (legs, thighs, or a combination)
- 4-5 guajillo chilies, dried
- 2 tomatoes, diced
- 1 onion, chopped
- 4 cloves garlic, minced
- 2 bay leaves
- 1 teaspoon cumin powder
- 1 teaspoon dried oregano
- 1/2 teaspoon ground coriander
- 1/2 teaspoon black pepper
- Salt to taste
- 2 tablespoons vegetable oil
- 4 cups chicken broth
- Fresh cilantro for garnish (optional)
- Lime wedges for serving

Instructions:

Prepare the Guajillo Chilies:
- Remove the stems and seeds from the guajillo chilies. Toast them in a dry skillet over medium heat for about 1-2 minutes, being careful not to burn them. Place the chilies in a bowl and cover with hot water. Allow them to soak for 15-20 minutes until they become soft.

Make the Guajillo Sauce:
- In a blender, combine the soaked guajillo chilies, diced tomatoes, minced garlic, cumin powder, dried oregano, ground coriander, black pepper, and a pinch of salt. Blend until you have a smooth sauce.

Brown the Chicken:
- In a large pot or Dutch oven, heat vegetable oil over medium-high heat. Brown the chicken pieces on all sides. This step adds flavor to the stew.

Saute Onions:
- Add chopped onions to the pot and sauté until they become translucent.

Add Guajillo Sauce:

- Pour the guajillo chili sauce over the browned chicken and onions. Stir to coat the chicken evenly with the sauce.

Add Chicken Broth:
- Pour in the chicken broth and add bay leaves. Bring the mixture to a boil.

Simmer:
- Reduce the heat to low, cover the pot, and let it simmer for about 30-40 minutes or until the chicken is cooked through and tender. Stir occasionally.

Adjust Seasoning:
- Taste the stew and adjust the seasoning with salt if needed.

Serve:
- Remove the bay leaves and discard them. Serve the guajillo chicken stew in bowls, garnished with fresh cilantro if desired. Serve with lime wedges on the side.

Enjoy this flavorful and aromatic Guajillo Chicken Stew with rice, tortillas, or your favorite side dishes. The guajillo chili imparts a rich and mildly spicy flavor to the chicken, making it a delightful and satisfying meal.

**Huitlacoche Quesadillas**

Ingredients:

- 1 cup huitlacoche, cleaned and chopped
- 1 small onion, finely chopped
- 2 cloves garlic, minced
- 1 tablespoon vegetable oil
- Salt and pepper to taste
- 8 small corn tortillas
- 2 cups Oaxaca cheese, shredded (or use shredded mozzarella or another melting cheese)
- Fresh cilantro, chopped, for garnish (optional)
- Lime wedges for serving

Instructions:

Prepare Huitlacoche:
- Clean the huitlacoche by wiping off any excess dirt. Chop it into small pieces.

Saute Huitlacoche Filling:
- In a skillet, heat vegetable oil over medium heat. Add chopped onion and minced garlic, sautéing until the onion becomes translucent.

Cook Huitlacoche:
- Add the chopped huitlacoche to the skillet. Cook for about 5-7 minutes, stirring occasionally, until it releases its moisture and cooks down.

Season:
- Season the huitlacoche mixture with salt and pepper to taste. Continue cooking until any excess liquid has evaporated, and the mixture is well-cooked.

Warm Tortillas:
- Heat the corn tortillas on a griddle or in a dry skillet until they are pliable. Keep them warm in a tortilla warmer or wrap them in a clean kitchen towel.

Assemble Quesadillas:
- On half of each tortilla, spread a portion of the huitlacoche mixture, leaving a border around the edges. Sprinkle a generous amount of shredded Oaxaca cheese on top of the huitlacoche.

Fold and Cook:
- Fold the tortillas in half, creating a half-moon shape. Press down gently with a spatula.

Cook Until Cheese Melts:
- Place the folded quesadillas on the griddle or skillet and cook for 2-3 minutes on each side, or until the cheese is melted, and the tortillas are golden brown.

Serve:
- Remove from heat and cut the quesadillas into wedges. Serve them hot, garnished with fresh cilantro if desired, and lime wedges on the side.

Enjoy these huitlacoche quesadillas as a unique and flavorful dish. They make for a tasty snack or light meal, and the earthy flavor of huitlacoche pairs wonderfully with the melted cheese and warm tortillas.

**Barbacoa**

Ingredients:

- 3 lbs beef chuck or beef cheek, cut into large chunks
- 3 cloves garlic, minced
- 2 teaspoons ground cumin
- 2 teaspoons dried oregano
- 1 teaspoon ground cloves
- 1 teaspoon ground cinnamon
- 1 teaspoon paprika
- 1 teaspoon salt (adjust to taste)
- 1/2 teaspoon black pepper
- 2-3 dried ancho chilies, stems and seeds removed
- 2-3 dried guajillo chilies, stems and seeds removed
- 1/2 cup apple cider vinegar
- 1/2 cup beef or vegetable broth
- 2 bay leaves
- Corn tortillas, for serving
- Fresh cilantro, diced onions, lime wedges, and salsa for garnish

Instructions:

Prepare the Dried Chilies:
- Toast the dried ancho and guajillo chilies in a dry skillet over medium heat for 1-2 minutes until fragrant. Soak them in hot water for about 15-20 minutes until softened. Reserve the soaking liquid.

Make the Adobo Sauce:
- In a blender, combine the soaked chilies, minced garlic, ground cumin, dried oregano, ground cloves, ground cinnamon, paprika, salt, black pepper, apple cider vinegar, and 1/2 cup of the soaking liquid. Blend until you have a smooth adobo sauce.

Marinate the Meat:
- Place the beef chunks in a large bowl and coat them with the adobo sauce. Cover the bowl and let the meat marinate in the refrigerator for at least 2 hours or overnight for more flavor.

Preheat the Oven:
- Preheat your oven to 325°F (163°C).

Cook the Barbacoa:

- Transfer the marinated beef and adobo sauce to a large oven-safe pot or a slow cooker. Add beef or vegetable broth, bay leaves, and mix well. Cover the pot.

Slow Cook:
- Cook the barbacoa in the preheated oven for about 3-4 hours, or until the meat is tender and easily shreds with a fork. If using a slow cooker, set it on low for 6-8 hours.

Shred the Meat:
- Once cooked, remove the bay leaves and shred the meat using two forks.

Serve:
- Serve the barbacoa on warm corn tortillas. Garnish with diced onions, fresh cilantro, and a squeeze of lime juice. You can also serve it with your favorite salsa or hot sauce.

Enjoy your homemade barbacoa as tacos, burritos, or in any other way you prefer! The slow-cooking process and flavorful spices make this dish incredibly tender and delicious.

**Salsa Roja Shrimp**

Ingredients:

- 1 lb large shrimp, peeled and deveined
- 2 cups Salsa Roja (homemade or store-bought)
- 2 tablespoons olive oil
- 1 onion, finely chopped
- 2 cloves garlic, minced
- 1 teaspoon ground cumin
- 1 teaspoon smoked paprika
- Salt and black pepper to taste
- Fresh cilantro, chopped, for garnish
- Lime wedges for serving
- Cooked rice or tortillas for serving

Instructions:

Prepare the Shrimp:
- If the shrimp are frozen, thaw them in cold water. Peel and devein the shrimp, leaving the tails on or removing them based on your preference.

Season the Shrimp:
- In a bowl, season the shrimp with ground cumin, smoked paprika, salt, and black pepper. Toss to coat the shrimp evenly with the spices.

Sauté Onion and Garlic:
- In a large skillet or pan, heat olive oil over medium heat. Add finely chopped onion and sauté until it becomes translucent.

Cook Shrimp:
- Add minced garlic to the skillet and cook for about 30 seconds until fragrant. Add the seasoned shrimp to the pan and cook for 2-3 minutes on each side or until they turn pink and opaque.

Add Salsa Roja:
- Pour in the Salsa Roja over the cooked shrimp. Stir well to coat the shrimp in the salsa.

Simmer:
- Reduce the heat to low and let the shrimp simmer in the salsa for an additional 5-7 minutes, allowing the flavors to meld and the shrimp to absorb the salsa.

Adjust Seasoning:
- Taste the dish and adjust the seasoning with salt and pepper if needed.

Serve:
- Serve the Salsa Roja Shrimp over cooked rice or inside warm tortillas for tacos. Garnish with chopped fresh cilantro and serve with lime wedges on the side.

This Salsa Roja Shrimp dish is versatile and can be enjoyed in various ways. The flavorful salsa adds a spicy kick to the succulent shrimp, making it a delicious and quick meal option. Customize the spiciness based on your preference and enjoy the vibrant flavors!

**Cochinita Pibil Tacos**

Ingredients:

For the Cochinita Pibil:

- 2 lbs pork shoulder, cut into chunks
- 4 tablespoons achiote paste
- 4 tablespoons orange juice
- 2 tablespoons lime juice
- 4 cloves garlic, minced
- 1 teaspoon ground cumin
- 1 teaspoon dried oregano
- 1/2 teaspoon ground cinnamon
- Salt to taste
- Banana leaves or aluminum foil for wrapping

For Tacos:

- Corn tortillas
- Pickled red onions (thinly sliced red onions marinated in vinegar, salt, and a pinch of sugar)
- Fresh cilantro, chopped
- Lime wedges
- Salsa (optional)

Instructions:

Marinate the Pork:
- In a bowl, mix together achiote paste, orange juice, lime juice, minced garlic, ground cumin, dried oregano, ground cinnamon, and salt. This is your marinade.
- Coat the pork chunks in the marinade, ensuring they are well covered. Marinate for at least 4 hours, preferably overnight in the refrigerator.

Prepare Banana Leaves or Aluminum Foil:
- If using banana leaves, pass them over an open flame or quickly warm them in a dry skillet to make them pliable.

- Place a portion of the marinated pork in the center of a banana leaf or aluminum foil. Wrap it tightly, creating a packet.

Slow Cook the Cochinita Pibil:
- Preheat your oven to 325°F (163°C).
- Place the wrapped cochinita pibil packets in a baking dish and bake for 3-4 hours or until the pork is tender and easily shreds with a fork.

Assemble Tacos:
- Heat corn tortillas on a griddle or in a dry skillet.
- Unwrap the cochinita pibil and shred the pork using two forks.
- Assemble tacos with a generous portion of cochinita pibil on each tortilla.

Add Toppings:
- Top the tacos with pickled red onions, chopped fresh cilantro, and a squeeze of lime juice. Optionally, add your favorite salsa for extra flavor.

Serve:
- Serve Cochinita Pibil Tacos immediately while the tortillas are warm and the pork is hot. Offer lime wedges on the side for extra zing.

Enjoy these Cochinita Pibil Tacos with their rich, flavorful pork, and the vibrant combination of pickled onions, cilantro, and lime. It's a classic Mexican dish that's sure to satisfy your taco cravings.

**Alambre**

Ingredients:

- 1 lb thinly sliced beef (skirt steak or sirloin works well)
- 1 bell pepper, thinly sliced
- 1 onion, thinly sliced
- 2 tablespoons vegetable oil
- 2 cloves garlic, minced
- 1-2 jalapeños, sliced (adjust to your spice preference)
- Salt and pepper to taste
- 1 cup shredded Oaxaca cheese or Monterrey Jack cheese
- Corn tortillas, for serving
- Fresh cilantro, chopped, for garnish (optional)
- Lime wedges for serving

Instructions:

Prepare the Meat:
- Season the thinly sliced beef with salt and pepper.

Sauté Vegetables:
- In a large skillet or pan, heat vegetable oil over medium-high heat. Add sliced bell peppers, onions, and minced garlic. Sauté until the vegetables are softened and slightly caramelized.

Cook the Beef:
- Push the sautéed vegetables to one side of the skillet and add the seasoned beef slices. Cook the beef until it's browned and cooked through, stirring occasionally. Ensure not to overcook to keep the beef tender.

Combine and Season:
- Combine the cooked beef with the sautéed vegetables. Add sliced jalapeños and continue cooking for an additional 2-3 minutes. Adjust the seasoning if needed.

Melt Cheese:
- Sprinkle the shredded cheese over the meat and vegetables. Cover the skillet with a lid and let it melt for a couple of minutes until the cheese is gooey and melted.

Assemble Alambre Tacos:

- Warm the corn tortillas on a griddle or in a dry skillet.
- Spoon the alambre mixture onto each tortilla.

Garnish and Serve:
- Garnish with chopped fresh cilantro if desired. Serve Alambre tacos immediately with lime wedges on the side.

Alambre is a versatile dish, and you can customize it by adding other ingredients like mushrooms, bacon, or different types of cheese. It's a flavorful and satisfying option for taco night or a quick and delicious meal.

**Mexican Street Corn Soup**

Ingredients:

- 4 cups corn kernels (fresh or frozen)
- 1 tablespoon vegetable oil
- 1 onion, finely chopped
- 3 cloves garlic, minced
- 1 teaspoon ground cumin
- 1 teaspoon chili powder
- 1/2 teaspoon smoked paprika
- 4 cups chicken or vegetable broth
- 1 cup milk (whole or 2%)
- 1 cup cotija cheese, crumbled (reserve some for garnish)
- 1/2 cup sour cream
- Juice of 1 lime
- Salt and black pepper to taste
- Fresh cilantro, chopped, for garnish
- Additional chili powder or paprika for sprinkling
- Lime wedges for serving

Instructions:

Cook the Corn:
- If using fresh corn, grill or boil the corn on the cob until cooked. Cut the kernels off the cob. If using frozen corn, thaw it.

Sauté Onions and Garlic:
- In a large pot, heat vegetable oil over medium heat. Add finely chopped onions and sauté until translucent. Add minced garlic and cook for an additional 1-2 minutes.

Spice Mixture:
- Stir in ground cumin, chili powder, and smoked paprika. Cook for a couple of minutes to toast the spices.

Add Corn and Broth:
- Add the corn kernels to the pot and pour in the chicken or vegetable broth. Bring the mixture to a simmer and cook for about 10-15 minutes.

Blend the Soup:
- Using an immersion blender or by transferring the mixture to a blender, puree the soup until smooth. Be cautious when blending hot liquids.

Finish the Soup:
- Return the blended soup to the pot over medium heat. Stir in milk, crumbled cotija cheese, sour cream, and lime juice. Season with salt and black pepper to taste.

Simmer:
- Allow the soup to simmer for an additional 10-15 minutes, letting the flavors meld.

Serve:
- Ladle the soup into bowls. Garnish with reserved cotija cheese, chopped fresh cilantro, and a sprinkle of chili powder or smoked paprika. Serve with lime wedges on the side.

Enjoy this Mexican Street Corn Soup as a delicious and warming dish that brings the flavors of elote to your table in a comforting soup form. Serve it with crusty bread or tortilla chips for a complete meal.

**Tinga de Pollo**

Ingredients:

- 2 lbs boneless, skinless chicken breasts or thighs, cooked and shredded
- 2 tablespoons vegetable oil
- 1 large onion, thinly sliced
- 3 cloves garlic, minced
- 2 chipotle peppers in adobo sauce, chopped (adjust to taste)
- 1 can (14 oz) diced tomatoes
- 1 teaspoon dried oregano
- 1 teaspoon ground cumin
- 1 teaspoon smoked paprika
- Salt and pepper to taste
- 1/2 cup chicken broth
- 2 bay leaves
- Corn tortillas, for serving
- Garnishes: chopped cilantro, crumbled queso fresco, sliced radishes, lime wedges

Instructions:

Cook and Shred Chicken:
- Cook the chicken breasts or thighs until fully cooked. You can boil, bake, or use a rotisserie chicken. Shred the cooked chicken and set it aside.

Sauté Onions and Garlic:
- In a large skillet, heat vegetable oil over medium heat. Add thinly sliced onions and cook until they become translucent. Add minced garlic and cook for an additional minute.

Add Chipotle Peppers:
- Stir in chopped chipotle peppers in adobo sauce. Adjust the amount based on your spice preference.

Tomato Sauce:
- Pour in the diced tomatoes, including the juice. Use a spoon to break down the tomatoes if they are whole. Cook for a few minutes until the tomatoes start to break down.

Seasoning:
- Add dried oregano, ground cumin, smoked paprika, salt, and pepper. Mix well to combine.

Combine with Shredded Chicken:
- Add the shredded chicken to the skillet and mix it with the tomato and spice mixture.

Add Chicken Broth and Bay Leaves:
- Pour in the chicken broth and add bay leaves. Stir everything together and let it simmer for about 15-20 minutes to allow the flavors to meld.

Adjust Seasoning:
- Taste the tinga de pollo and adjust the seasoning if needed. You can add more salt, pepper, or chipotle peppers for extra heat.

Serve:
- Warm the corn tortillas. Spoon the tinga de pollo onto the tortillas. Garnish with chopped cilantro, crumbled queso fresco, sliced radishes, and lime wedges.

Enjoy Tinga de Pollo as a flavorful taco filling or serve it over rice for a delicious and satisfying meal. It's a versatile dish with a perfect balance of smoky, spicy, and savory flavors.

**Tacos de Birria**

Ingredients:

For the Birria:

- 3 lbs beef chuck roast, cut into chunks (or goat meat if preferred)
- 4 dried guajillo chilies, stems and seeds removed
- 2 dried ancho chilies, stems and seeds removed
- 3 cloves garlic, minced
- 1 onion, chopped
- 1 tablespoon dried oregano
- 1 teaspoon ground cumin
- 1/2 teaspoon ground cinnamon
- Salt and pepper to taste
- 4 cups beef broth
- 2 bay leaves

For the Tacos:

- Corn tortillas
- Chopped white onion
- Chopped fresh cilantro
- Lime wedges
- Salsa (optional)

Instructions:

Prepare the Chilies:
- Toast the dried guajillo and ancho chilies in a dry skillet over medium heat for 1-2 minutes until fragrant. Soak them in hot water for about 15-20 minutes or until softened.

Make the Birria Paste:
- In a blender, combine the soaked chilies, minced garlic, chopped onion, dried oregano, ground cumin, ground cinnamon, salt, and pepper. Blend until you have a smooth paste.

Marinate the Meat:

- Place the beef chunks in a large bowl and coat them with the birria paste. Cover and let it marinate for at least 2 hours or overnight in the refrigerator.

Cook the Birria:
- Preheat your oven to 325°F (163°C).
- Transfer the marinated meat to a large Dutch oven or oven-safe pot. Add beef broth and bay leaves. Cover the pot and place it in the preheated oven. Cook for 3-4 hours or until the meat is tender and easily shreds.

Shred the Meat:
- Once cooked, shred the meat using two forks. Remove any excess fat.

Serve Tacos:
- Heat corn tortillas on a griddle or in a dry skillet.
- Fill each tortilla with the shredded birria meat.

Garnish and Serve:
- Top the tacos with chopped white onion, fresh cilantro, and a squeeze of lime juice. Serve with salsa on the side if desired.

Tacos de Birria are often served with a side of the rich broth from the cooking process for dipping, known as consomé. Ladle some consomé into small cups for a delightful dipping experience. Enjoy these flavorful and comforting Tacos de Birria for a delicious taste of Mexican cuisine!

**Sopa de Lima**

Ingredients:

- 2 tablespoons vegetable oil
- 1 onion, finely chopped
- 2 cloves garlic, minced
- 2 tomatoes, diced
- 1-2 jalapeños, finely chopped (adjust to your spice preference)
- 1 teaspoon ground cumin
- 1 teaspoon dried oregano
- 6 cups chicken broth
- 2 chicken breasts, cooked and shredded
- 2 limes, juiced
- Salt and black pepper to taste
- 4 corn tortillas, cut into strips
- Vegetable oil for frying tortilla strips
- Avocado slices, for garnish
- Fresh cilantro, chopped, for garnish

Instructions:

Prepare Tortilla Strips:
- Heat vegetable oil in a pan. Fry the tortilla strips until golden brown and crispy. Remove them from the oil and place them on a paper towel to drain excess oil. Set aside.

Make the Base:
- In a large pot, heat 2 tablespoons of vegetable oil over medium heat. Add finely chopped onion and sauté until translucent. Add minced garlic and cook for an additional minute.

Add Vegetables and Spices:
- Stir in diced tomatoes, chopped jalapeños, ground cumin, and dried oregano. Cook for a few minutes until the tomatoes are soft.

Pour in Chicken Broth:
- Pour in the chicken broth and bring the mixture to a simmer. Let it cook for about 10-15 minutes to allow the flavors to meld.

Add Shredded Chicken:
- Add the shredded chicken to the pot and let it simmer for an additional 5 minutes.

Season with Lime Juice:
- Squeeze the juice of two limes into the soup. Adjust the lime juice, salt, and black pepper to your taste.

Serve:
- Ladle the Sopa de Lima into bowls. Garnish with fried tortilla strips, avocado slices, and chopped fresh cilantro.

Sopa de Lima is known for its vibrant flavors, and the addition of lime gives it a refreshing and tangy taste. It's a comforting soup that can be enjoyed on its own or as part of a larger meal. Serve it with warm tortillas or crusty bread for a complete experience.

**Chicken Tinga Tostadas**

Ingredients:

For the Chicken Tinga:

- 2 cups shredded cooked chicken (rotisserie chicken works well)
- 1 onion, finely sliced
- 2 cloves garlic, minced
- 1 can (14 oz) diced tomatoes
- 2-3 chipotle peppers in adobo sauce, chopped (adjust to taste)
- 1 teaspoon dried oregano
- 1 teaspoon ground cumin
- 1/2 teaspoon smoked paprika
- Salt and pepper to taste
- 2 tablespoons vegetable oil

For Tostadas:

- Tostada shells (store-bought or homemade)
- Refried beans (optional)
- Shredded lettuce
- Diced tomatoes
- Crumbled queso fresco or shredded cheese
- Avocado slices
- Fresh cilantro, chopped
- Lime wedges

Instructions:

Prepare the Chicken Tinga:
- In a blender, combine the diced tomatoes, chopped chipotle peppers, dried oregano, ground cumin, smoked paprika, salt, and pepper. Blend until you have a smooth sauce.

Sauté Onions and Garlic:

- In a large skillet, heat vegetable oil over medium heat. Add sliced onions and cook until they become translucent. Add minced garlic and cook for an additional minute.

Add Shredded Chicken:
- Add the shredded chicken to the skillet and sauté for a couple of minutes, allowing the chicken to absorb the flavors.

Pour in the Tinga Sauce:
- Pour the blended sauce over the chicken in the skillet. Stir well to coat the chicken in the tinga sauce. Simmer for about 10-15 minutes, allowing the flavors to meld.

Assemble Tostadas:
- If using refried beans, spread a thin layer on each tostada shell.
- Spoon a generous portion of the chicken tinga onto each tostada.

Top with Fresh Ingredients:
- Top the chicken tinga with shredded lettuce, diced tomatoes, crumbled queso fresco or shredded cheese, avocado slices, and chopped fresh cilantro.

Serve:
- Serve the Chicken Tinga Tostadas with lime wedges on the side.

Enjoy these Chicken Tinga Tostadas as a delightful and satisfying meal. The smoky and spicy flavor of the tinga sauce combined with the fresh toppings makes for a perfect combination on crispy tostada shells.

# Huachinango a la Veracruzana (Veracruz-Style Red Snapper)

Ingredients:

- 2 whole red snappers, cleaned and scaled (about 1.5 to 2 lbs each)
- Salt and black pepper to taste
- 1/2 cup all-purpose flour, for dredging
- 3 tablespoons vegetable oil
- 1 onion, finely chopped
- 3 cloves garlic, minced
- 1 bell pepper (red or green), thinly sliced
- 1 can (14 oz) diced tomatoes, drained (reserve the juice)
- 1/2 cup green olives, pitted and sliced
- 2 tablespoons capers, drained
- 1 teaspoon dried oregano
- 1/2 teaspoon dried thyme
- 1 bay leaf
- 1/2 cup chicken or vegetable broth
- 1/2 cup dry white wine
- Fresh cilantro, chopped, for garnish
- Lime wedges for serving
- Cooked white rice, for serving

Instructions:

Prepare the Red Snapper:
- Rinse the red snappers under cold water and pat them dry with paper towels. Season the inside and outside of the fish with salt and black pepper.

Dredge in Flour:
- Dredge the red snappers in flour, shaking off any excess.

Pan-Fry the Red Snapper:
- In a large skillet, heat vegetable oil over medium-high heat. Add the red snappers and cook for about 3-4 minutes on each side or until they are golden brown. Remove them from the skillet and set aside.

Make the Veracruzana Sauce:

- In the same skillet, add chopped onion and sauté until it becomes translucent. Add minced garlic and sliced bell pepper, cooking for an additional 2 minutes.
- Stir in diced tomatoes, green olives, capers, dried oregano, dried thyme, and the bay leaf. Cook for another 3-4 minutes.

Add Liquid Ingredients:
- Pour in the chicken or vegetable broth and white wine. Add the reserved juice from the diced tomatoes. Bring the mixture to a simmer.

Simmer the Red Snapper:
- Return the pan-fried red snappers to the skillet, spooning the Veracruzana sauce over them. Cover the skillet and let it simmer for about 15-20 minutes or until the fish is cooked through.

Garnish and Serve:
- Garnish the Huachinango a la Veracruzana with chopped fresh cilantro. Serve the red snapper over cooked white rice with lime wedges on the side.

Enjoy Huachinango a la Veracruzana, a dish celebrated for its vibrant and aromatic flavors. The combination of tomatoes, olives, capers, and herbs creates a delicious sauce that complements the tender and flaky red snapper.

**Tacos de Carnitas con Salsa Verde**

Ingredients:

For the Carnitas:

- 2 lbs pork shoulder, cut into chunks
- 1 onion, chopped
- 4 cloves garlic, minced
- 1 teaspoon ground cumin
- 1 teaspoon dried oregano
- 1 teaspoon smoked paprika
- Salt and black pepper to taste
- 2 bay leaves
- 1 orange, juiced
- 1 lime, juiced
- 2 tablespoons vegetable oil

For the Salsa Verde:

- 6 tomatillos, husked and rinsed
- 1 jalapeño pepper (adjust to taste)
- 1/2 onion, chopped
- 2 cloves garlic
- 1 cup fresh cilantro leaves
- 1 lime, juiced
- Salt to taste

For Tacos:

- Corn tortillas
- Chopped white onion
- Chopped fresh cilantro
- Lime wedges

Instructions:

For the Carnitas:

### Season the Pork:
- In a bowl, combine the pork chunks with chopped onion, minced garlic, ground cumin, dried oregano, smoked paprika, salt, and black pepper. Mix well to coat the pork evenly with the spices.

### Marinate:
- Marinate the pork in the refrigerator for at least 2 hours or preferably overnight to allow the flavors to meld.

### Cook the Carnitas:
- In a large, heavy-bottomed pot, heat vegetable oil over medium-high heat. Add the marinated pork and sear on all sides until browned.

### Add Citrus Juice:
- Squeeze the juice of one orange and one lime over the browned pork. Add bay leaves. Stir well.

### Simmer:
- Lower the heat, cover the pot, and let the pork simmer for 2-3 hours or until the meat is tender and easily shreds with a fork.

### Crisp the Carnitas (Optional):
- If desired, transfer the shredded pork to a baking sheet and broil for a few minutes to crisp up the edges.

For the Salsa Verde:

### Roast Tomatillos and Jalapeño:
- Roast the tomatillos and jalapeño in a dry skillet over medium-high heat until they are charred on all sides.

### Blend Ingredients:
- In a blender, combine the roasted tomatillos, jalapeño, chopped onion, garlic, cilantro, lime juice, and salt. Blend until you have a smooth salsa verde.

Assemble Tacos:

### Warm Tortillas:
- Heat corn tortillas on a griddle or in a dry skillet until warm.

### Fill Tacos:
- Fill each tortilla with a generous portion of carnitas.

Top with Salsa Verde:
- Spoon salsa verde over the carnitas.

Add Toppings:
- Garnish with chopped white onion, fresh cilantro, and a squeeze of lime juice.

Serve:
- Serve Tacos de Carnitas con Salsa Verde immediately. Enjoy with lime wedges on the side.

These Tacos de Carnitas con Salsa Verde offer a delightful combination of tender and flavorful pork with the freshness and zing of the green salsa. Customize your toppings and savor the deliciousness of authentic Mexican street-style tacos!

**Pescado Zarandeado**

Ingredients:

For the Adobo Sauce:

- 3 dried guajillo chilies, stems and seeds removed
- 2 dried ancho chilies, stems and seeds removed
- 3 cloves garlic
- 1/2 small onion, roughly chopped
- 1 teaspoon dried oregano
- 1 teaspoon ground cumin
- 1/2 teaspoon ground black pepper
- 1/2 cup orange juice
- 1/4 cup lime juice
- Salt to taste
- 2 tablespoons vegetable oil

For the Fish:

- 1 whole fish (red snapper or sea bass work well), cleaned and butterflied
- Salt and black pepper to taste
- Vegetable oil for grilling
- Lime wedges for serving
- Chopped fresh cilantro for garnish

Instructions:

For the Adobo Sauce:

Prepare the Chilies:
- Toast the dried guajillo and ancho chilies in a dry skillet over medium heat for 1-2 minutes until fragrant. Soak them in hot water for about 15-20 minutes or until softened.

Make the Adobo Paste:
- In a blender, combine the soaked chilies, garlic, chopped onion, dried oregano, ground cumin, black pepper, orange juice, lime juice, and salt. Blend until you have a smooth adobo paste.

Cook the Adobo Sauce:

- Heat vegetable oil in a saucepan over medium heat. Add the blended adobo paste and cook for 5-7 minutes, stirring frequently, until the flavors meld and the sauce thickens slightly. Set aside.

For the Fish:

Prepare the Fish:
- Clean and butterfly the whole fish. Make deep cuts on both sides of the fish to allow the adobo sauce to penetrate.

Marinate the Fish:
- Generously brush the fish with the adobo sauce, making sure to get the marinade into the cuts. Allow the fish to marinate for at least 1-2 hours in the refrigerator.

Preheat the Grill:
- Preheat a grill to medium-high heat.

Grill the Fish:
- Brush the grill grates with vegetable oil to prevent sticking. Place the marinated fish on the grill and cook for about 10-15 minutes on each side or until the fish is cooked through and has a nice char.

Serve:
- Transfer the grilled fish to a serving platter. Garnish with chopped fresh cilantro and serve with lime wedges on the side.

Enjoy Pescado Zarandeado with its smoky, flavorful, and slightly spicy taste. This dish is often enjoyed with warm tortillas, rice, and grilled vegetables for a complete and delicious meal.

**Tacos de Rajas con Queso**

Ingredients:

- 4 large poblano peppers
- 1 tablespoon vegetable oil
- 1 large onion, thinly sliced
- 2 cloves garlic, minced
- 1 cup Mexican melting cheese (such as Oaxaca, asadero, or Monterey Jack), shredded
- Salt and pepper to taste
- Corn tortillas
- Fresh cilantro, chopped, for garnish
- Lime wedges for serving

Instructions:

Roast and Peel Poblano Peppers:
- Place poblano peppers on a hot grill or directly over a gas flame on the stove. Roast until the skin is charred and blistered, turning them occasionally. Once charred, transfer the peppers to a plastic bag and let them steam for about 10 minutes. Peel off the skin, remove the seeds and membranes, and slice the peppers into thin strips (rajas).

Sauté Onions and Garlic:
- In a skillet, heat vegetable oil over medium heat. Add thinly sliced onions and cook until softened and lightly caramelized. Add minced garlic and cook for an additional minute.

Add Poblano Strips:
- Add the poblano strips (rajas) to the skillet with the sautéed onions and garlic. Cook for a few minutes until the peppers are tender.

Melt Cheese:
- Reduce the heat to low and sprinkle the shredded Mexican melting cheese over the poblano strips. Stir gently until the cheese is melted and well combined with the peppers.

Season:
- Season the mixture with salt and pepper to taste. Adjust the seasoning according to your preference.

Warm Tortillas:

- Heat corn tortillas on a griddle or in a dry skillet until warm and pliable.

Assemble Tacos:
- Spoon the rajas con queso mixture onto each warm tortilla.

Garnish and Serve:
- Garnish with chopped fresh cilantro and serve the Tacos de Rajas con Queso immediately. Serve with lime wedges on the side.

These tacos are simple yet incredibly flavorful, showcasing the smoky richness of the roasted poblanos and the gooey goodness of melted cheese. They can be enjoyed as a vegetarian option or accompanied by grilled meat for a heartier version.

**Pambazos**

Ingredients:

For the Guajillo Pepper Sauce:

- 4-5 dried guajillo peppers, stems and seeds removed
- 2 cloves garlic
- 1/2 teaspoon dried oregano
- Salt to taste
- 2 cups water

For the Filling:

- 4 medium-sized potatoes, peeled, boiled, and sliced
- 1 lb Mexican chorizo, cooked and crumbled
- 1 cup shredded lettuce
- Mexican crema or sour cream
- Queso fresco, crumbled (optional)
- Vegetable oil for frying
- 4 pambazo rolls (if unavailable, use bolillos or another type of soft sandwich roll)

Instructions:

For the Guajillo Pepper Sauce:

Prepare the Guajillo Peppers:
- Remove the stems and seeds from the dried guajillo peppers.

Make the Sauce:
- In a saucepan, combine the guajillo peppers, garlic, dried oregano, salt, and water. Bring to a boil, then reduce the heat and simmer for about 10-15 minutes until the peppers are soft.

Blend the Sauce:
- Transfer the sauce ingredients to a blender and blend until smooth. Strain the sauce to remove any solids.

Assembling the Pambazos:

Prep the Rolls:
- Cut each pambazo roll in half without completely separating the halves.

Dip the Bread:
- Using a brush or your hands, generously dip each roll into the guajillo pepper sauce, ensuring it is well-coated.

Cook the Rolls:
- In a skillet or griddle, heat a bit of vegetable oil over medium heat. Place the dipped rolls on the hot surface and cook until they are slightly crispy and have absorbed the flavor of the sauce.

Fill the Pambazos:
- Open the rolls and fill each one with sliced potatoes, crumbled chorizo, shredded lettuce, crema, and crumbled queso fresco if desired.

Serve:
- Close the pambazos and serve them immediately while warm.

Enjoy Pambazos as a flavorful and satisfying street food experience. The combination of the spiced guajillo pepper sauce, savory chorizo, and creamy crema makes for a delightful and unique Mexican sandwich.

**Chorizo and Potato Tacos**

Ingredients:

- 1 lb Mexican chorizo
- 4 medium-sized potatoes, peeled and diced
- 1 small onion, finely chopped
- 2 cloves garlic, minced
- Salt and pepper to taste
- Corn tortillas
- Chopped fresh cilantro, for garnish
- Lime wedges, for serving
- Salsa or hot sauce (optional)

Instructions:

Cook the Chorizo:
- In a skillet over medium heat, remove the chorizo from its casing and cook it, breaking it apart with a spoon as it cooks. Cook until the chorizo is browned and fully cooked.

Add Onions and Garlic:
- Add finely chopped onions and minced garlic to the cooked chorizo. Sauté for a few minutes until the onions are translucent.

Add Potatoes:
- Add the diced potatoes to the skillet with the chorizo mixture. Stir well to coat the potatoes in the flavorful chorizo and onion mixture.

Cook Potatoes:
- Cook the potatoes over medium heat, stirring occasionally, until they are tender. This may take around 15-20 minutes. Season with salt and pepper to taste.

Warm Tortillas:
- While the potatoes are cooking, warm the corn tortillas on a griddle or in a dry skillet.

Assemble Tacos:
- Spoon the chorizo and potato mixture onto each warm tortilla.

Garnish and Serve:

- Garnish the tacos with chopped fresh cilantro. Serve the tacos with lime wedges on the side for squeezing over the top. You can also add salsa or hot sauce if desired.

Enjoy:
- Serve the Chorizo and Potato Tacos immediately. Enjoy the delicious combination of spicy chorizo and tender potatoes in each bite.

These tacos are versatile, and you can customize them with your favorite toppings such as diced onions, crumbled queso fresco, or sliced radishes. They make for a satisfying and flavorful meal, perfect for any taco night.

**Chicken Chiles Rellenos**

Ingredients:

For the Chicken Filling:

- 2 cups shredded cooked chicken (rotisserie chicken works well)
- 1 cup cooked rice
- 1/2 cup black beans, drained and rinsed
- 1/2 cup corn kernels (fresh or frozen)
- 1 cup shredded Monterey Jack or Mexican blend cheese
- 1 teaspoon ground cumin
- 1 teaspoon chili powder
- Salt and pepper to taste
- Fresh cilantro, chopped, for garnish

For the Chiles Rellenos:

- 4 large poblano peppers
- 1 cup all-purpose flour, for coating
- 3 large eggs, separated
- Salt and pepper to taste
- Vegetable oil, for frying

For the Tomato Sauce:

- 2 tablespoons vegetable oil
- 1 onion, chopped
- 2 cloves garlic, minced
- 1 can (14 oz) crushed tomatoes
- 1 teaspoon dried oregano
- 1 teaspoon ground cumin
- Salt and pepper to taste

Instructions:

For the Chicken Filling:

Prepare the Chicken Filling:
- In a bowl, combine shredded chicken, cooked rice, black beans, corn, shredded cheese, ground cumin, chili powder, salt, and pepper. Mix well to combine.

## For the Chiles Rellenos:

Roast and Peel Poblano Peppers:
- Place poblano peppers on a hot grill or directly over a gas flame on the stove. Roast until the skin is charred and blistered, turning them occasionally. Once charred, transfer the peppers to a plastic bag and let them steam for about 10 minutes. Peel off the skin, make a slit down one side, and remove the seeds and membranes.

Stuff the Peppers:
- Stuff each poblano pepper with the chicken filling, ensuring they are well-filled but can still be closed.

Coat in Flour:
- Roll each stuffed pepper in flour until evenly coated.

Prepare Egg Batter:
- In a bowl, beat the egg yolks until thick and pale. In a separate bowl, beat the egg whites until stiff peaks form. Gently fold the egg whites into the yolks. Season with salt and pepper.

Dip and Fry:
- Dip each flour-coated pepper into the egg batter, ensuring it's well-covered. In a large skillet, heat vegetable oil over medium-high heat. Fry the stuffed and battered peppers until golden brown on all sides. Place them on a paper towel to drain excess oil.

## For the Tomato Sauce:

Prepare the Tomato Sauce:
- In a saucepan, heat vegetable oil over medium heat. Add chopped onions and cook until softened. Add minced garlic and cook for an additional minute. Stir in crushed tomatoes, dried oregano, ground cumin, salt, and pepper. Simmer the sauce for about 10-15 minutes.

Serve:
- Spoon the tomato sauce over the fried Chicken Chiles Rellenos. Garnish with chopped fresh cilantro.

Enjoy Chicken Chiles Rellenos as a flavorful and satisfying meal. The combination of the savory chicken filling, roasted poblano peppers, and tangy tomato sauce makes for a delicious dish with authentic Mexican flavors.

**Sopes de Tinga**

Ingredients:

For the Tinga de Pollo:

- 2 cups shredded cooked chicken
- 1 onion, finely chopped
- 2 cloves garlic, minced
- 1 can (14 oz) diced tomatoes
- 2-3 chipotle peppers in adobo sauce, chopped (adjust to taste)
- 1 teaspoon dried oregano
- 1 teaspoon ground cumin
- Salt and pepper to taste
- 2 tablespoons vegetable oil

For the Sopes:

- 2 cups masa harina (corn masa flour)
- 1 1/4 cups warm water
- 1/2 teaspoon salt
- Vegetable oil for frying

Toppings:

- Refried beans
- Shredded lettuce
- Crumbled queso fresco
- Mexican crema or sour cream
- Sliced radishes
- Chopped fresh cilantro
- Lime wedges

Instructions:

For the Tinga de Pollo:

    Prepare the Tinga Sauce:

- In a blender, combine diced tomatoes, chopped chipotle peppers, minced garlic, dried oregano, ground cumin, salt, and pepper. Blend until you have a smooth sauce.

Cook the Tinga:
- In a skillet, heat vegetable oil over medium heat. Add finely chopped onions and cook until they become translucent. Add shredded chicken and pour the blended tinga sauce over the chicken. Cook for about 10-15 minutes, allowing the flavors to meld and the sauce to thicken. Adjust seasoning if needed.

For the Sopes:

Prepare the Masa Dough:
- In a large bowl, combine masa harina, warm water, and salt. Mix well until you have a soft and pliable dough. If needed, add a bit more water.

Form Sopes:
- Take golf ball-sized portions of the masa dough and shape them into small, thick discs, about 3 inches in diameter. Use your hands to create a slight rim around the edges.

Cook Sopes:
- In a skillet, heat vegetable oil over medium-high heat. Fry each masa disc on both sides until they are golden brown and cooked through. Drain excess oil on a paper towel.

Assemble Sopes:
- Spread a thin layer of refried beans on each sope. Top with a generous portion of tinga de pollo.

Add Toppings:
- Garnish the Sopes de Tinga with shredded lettuce, crumbled queso fresco, a drizzle of Mexican crema or sour cream, sliced radishes, and chopped fresh cilantro.

Serve:
- Serve the Sopes de Tinga with lime wedges on the side. Enjoy them while they are still warm.

Sopes de Tinga make for a delicious and visually appealing meal with a combination of textures and flavors. The crispy base, flavorful tinga de pollo, and vibrant toppings create a satisfying dish that's perfect for any occasion.

**Tacos de Marlin**

Ingredients:

For the Marlin:

- 1 lb marlin fillets, skinless and boneless
- Juice of 2 limes
- 2 tablespoons olive oil
- 2 cloves garlic, minced
- 1 teaspoon ground cumin
- 1 teaspoon dried oregano
- Salt and pepper to taste

For the Tacos:

- Corn tortillas
- Shredded cabbage or lettuce
- Pico de gallo (chopped tomatoes, onions, cilantro, and lime juice)
- Sliced radishes
- Avocado slices
- Fresh cilantro, chopped
- Lime wedges

Instructions:

Marinate the Marlin:
- In a bowl, mix lime juice, olive oil, minced garlic, ground cumin, dried oregano, salt, and pepper to create a marinade.
- Cut the marlin fillets into small, manageable pieces. Place the marlin in the marinade, ensuring each piece is well-coated. Let it marinate in the refrigerator for at least 30 minutes.

Cook the Marlin:
- Heat a grill or skillet over medium-high heat. Grill or sauté the marlin pieces for 2-3 minutes per side or until the fish is cooked through and has a nice sear. Be careful not to overcook, as marlin can become dry.

Warm Tortillas:
- Heat corn tortillas on a griddle or in a dry skillet until warm and pliable.

Assemble Tacos:

- Place a portion of the grilled marlin on each tortilla.

Add Toppings:
- Top the marlin with shredded cabbage or lettuce, pico de gallo, sliced radishes, avocado slices, and fresh cilantro.

Serve:
- Serve Tacos de Marlin with lime wedges on the side for squeezing over the top.

Enjoy these Tacos de Marlin as a delightful and fresh seafood option. The grilled marlin, combined with the crispness of the vegetables and the tanginess of the lime, creates a flavorful and satisfying taco experience.

**Churros with Chocolate Dipping Sauce**

Ingredients:

For the Churros:

- 1 cup water
- 2 1/2 tablespoons sugar
- 1/2 teaspoon salt
- 2 tablespoons vegetable oil
- 1 cup all-purpose flour
- Vegetable oil, for frying

For the Coating:

- 1/4 cup sugar
- 1 teaspoon ground cinnamon

For the Chocolate Dipping Sauce:

- 1/2 cup dark chocolate, chopped
- 1/2 cup heavy cream
- 1 tablespoon unsalted butter
- 1 teaspoon vanilla extract

Instructions:

For the Churros:

    Prepare Churro Dough:
- In a saucepan, combine water, sugar, salt, and vegetable oil. Bring to a boil over medium heat.
- Remove from heat and add the flour. Stir vigorously until the mixture forms a dough.

    Shape Churros:
- Transfer the dough to a piping bag fitted with a star tip. Pipe 4-6 inch long strips onto a parchment paper-lined tray. You can also pipe circles or shapes if desired.

    Heat Oil for Frying:
- In a deep pan, heat vegetable oil to 375°F (190°C).

    Fry Churros:

- Carefully place the churros in the hot oil and fry until golden brown, turning them for even cooking. This usually takes about 2-3 minutes.

Drain and Coat:
- Remove the churros with a slotted spoon and place them on a plate lined with paper towels to drain excess oil. While still warm, roll the churros in a mixture of sugar and ground cinnamon.

For the Chocolate Dipping Sauce:

Prepare Chocolate Sauce:
- In a heatproof bowl, combine chopped dark chocolate, heavy cream, and butter.

Melt Chocolate:
- Place the bowl over a pot of simmering water (double boiler) and stir until the chocolate is melted and the mixture is smooth.

Add Vanilla Extract:
- Remove from heat and stir in the vanilla extract.

Serve:
- Serve the churros warm with the chocolate dipping sauce on the side.

Enjoy these homemade churros with a rich and decadent chocolate dipping sauce. They're perfect for a sweet treat or as a delightful dessert for gatherings.

## Capirotada (Mexican Bread Pudding)

Ingredients:

- 6 slices of bolillo or French bread, toasted
- 2 cups shredded Oaxaca or Monterey Jack cheese
- 1 cup peanuts or chopped pecans
- 1 cup raisins
- 1 cup grated piloncillo (or brown sugar)
- 3 cinnamon sticks
- 4 cups water
- 1/2 cup unsalted butter
- Ground cinnamon for sprinkling

Instructions:

Prepare the Syrup:
- In a saucepan, combine grated piloncillo, cinnamon sticks, and water. Bring to a boil, then reduce the heat and simmer for about 10-15 minutes until the piloncillo is completely dissolved. Remove cinnamon sticks and set aside.

Assemble the Layers:
- Preheat your oven to 350°F (175°C).
- In a baking dish, layer half of the toasted bread slices, followed by half of the shredded cheese, half of the nuts, and half of the raisins.
- Repeat the layering with the remaining half of the ingredients.

Pour Syrup:
- Pour the piloncillo syrup over the layered ingredients, ensuring that the bread is well-soaked.

Dot with Butter:
- Cut the unsalted butter into small pieces and dot the top of the capirotada with the butter.

Bake:
- Cover the baking dish with aluminum foil and bake in the preheated oven for about 30 minutes. Then, uncover and bake for an additional 15-20 minutes until the top is golden brown.

Serve:
- Allow the capirotada to cool for a bit before serving. Sprinkle ground cinnamon on top for an extra touch.

Optional Additions:

- Some variations include adding sliced bananas or apples between the layers.
- You can also drizzle condensed milk or evaporated milk over the capirotada before serving.

Capirotada is known for its unique combination of sweet and savory flavors. It's a comforting and festive dessert that holds cultural significance during Lent and Holy Week in Mexican households. Enjoy it as a special treat with family and friends.

www.ingramcontent.com/pod-product-compliance
Lightning Source LLC
LaVergne TN
LVHW081556060526
838201LV00054B/1925